PRISONER OF JOY

Living in Christ's Fullness and Freedom

A Study of the Prison Epistles
(Ephesians, Philippians, Colossians, Philemon)

Jack W. Hayford
with
Joseph Snider

THOMAS NELSON PUBLISHERS
Nashville

Prisoner of Joy: Living in Christ's Fullness and Freedom
A Study of the Prison Epistles
Copyright © 1994 by Jack W. Hayford

All Scripture quotations are from:

The Holy Bible, New King James Version
Copyright © 1982 by Thomas Nelson, Inc.

The New King James Bible, New Testament
Copyright © 1979 by Thomas Nelson, Inc.
The New King James Bible, New Testament and Psalms
Copyright © 1980 by Thomas Nelson, Inc.

CONTENTS

Prisoner of Joy: Living in Christ's Fullness and Freedom (A Study of the Prison Epistles) is one of a series of study guides that focus exciting, discovery-geared coverage of Bible book and power themes—all prompting toward dynamic, Holy Spirit-filled living.

About the Executive Editor

JACK W. HAYFORD, noted pastor, teacher, writer, and composer, is the Executive Editor of the complete series, working with the publisher in the conceiving and developing of each of the books.

Dr. Hayford is Senior Pastor of The Church On The Way, the First Foursquare Church of Van Nuys, California. He and his wife, Anna, have four married children, all of whom are active in either pastoral ministry or vital church life. As General Editor of the *Spirit-Filled Life Bible,* Pastor Hayford led a four-year project, which has resulted in the availability of one of today's most practical and popular study Bibles. He is author of more than twenty books, including *A Passion for Fullness, The Beauty of Spiritual Language, Rebuilding the Real You,* and *Prayer Is Invading the Impossible.* His musical compositions number over four hundred songs, including the widely sung "Majesty."

About the Writer

JOSEPH SNIDER has worked in Christian ministry for twenty-two years. In addition to freelance writing and speaking, he worked three years with Young Life, served for seven years on the Christian Education faculty at Fort Wayne Bible College, and pastored churches in Indianapolis and Fort Wayne, Indiana. He currently enjoys part-time teaching at Franklin College in Franklin, Indiana. His writing includes material for Thomas Nelson Publishers, Moody Magazine, Union Gospel Press, and David C. Cook.

Married to Sally Snider, Joe has two children: Jenny is 21 and Ted is 18. They live in Indianapolis, Indiana. Joe earned a B.A. in English from Cedarville College in Cedarville, Ohio, and a Th.M. in Christian Education from Dallas Theological Seminary.

Of this contributor, the Executive Editor has remarked: "Joe Snider's strength and stability as a gracious, godly man comes through in his writing. His perceptive and practical way of pointing the way to truth inspires students of God's Word."

THE GIFT
THAT KEEPS ON GIVING

Who doesn't like presents? Whether they come wrapped in colorful paper and beautiful bows, or brown paper bags closed and tied at the top with old shoestring. Kids and adults of all ages love getting and opening presents.

But even this moment of surprise and pleasure can be marked by dread and fear. All it takes is for these words to appear: "Assembly Required. Instructions Enclosed." How we hate these words! They taunt us, tease us, beckon us to try to challenge them, all the while knowing that they have the upper hand. If we don't understand the instructions, or if we ignore them and try to put the gift together ourselves, more than likely we'll only assemble frustration and anger. What we felt about our great gift—all the joy, anticipation, and wonder—will vanish. And they will never return, at least not to that pristine state they had before we realized that *we* had to assemble our present with instructions *no consumer* will ever understand.

One of the most precious gifts God has given us is His Word, the Bible. Wrapped in the glory and sacrifice of His Son and delivered by the power and ministry of His Spirit, it is a treasured gift—one the family of God has preserved and protected for centuries as a family heirloom. It promises that it is the gift that keeps on giving, because the Giver it reveals is inexhaustible in His love and grace.

Tragically, though, fewer and fewer people, even those who number themselves among God's everlasting family, are opening this gift and seeking to understand what it's all about and how to use it. They often feel intimidated by it. It requires some assembly, and its instructions are hard to comprehend sometimes. How does the Bible fit together anyway?

What does Genesis have to do with Revelation? Who are Abraham and Moses, and what is their relationship to Jesus and Paul? And what about the works of the Law and the works of faith? What are they all about, and how do they fit together, if at all?

And what does this ancient Book have to say to us who are looking toward the twenty-first century? Will taking the time and energy to understand its instructions and to fit it all together really help you and me? Will it help us better understand who we are, what the future holds, how we can better live here and now? Will it really help us in our personal relationships, in our marriages and families, in our jobs? Can it give us more than just advice on how to handle crises? the death of a loved one? the financial fallout of losing a job? catastrophic illness? betrayal by a friend? the seduction of our values? the abuses of the heart and soul? Will it allay our fears and calm our restlessness and heal our wounds? Can it really get us in touch with the same power that gave birth to the universe? that parted the Red Sea? that raised Jesus from the stranglehold of the grave? Can we really find unconditional love, total forgiveness, and genuine healing in its pages?

Yes. Yes. Without a shred of doubt.

The *Spirit-Filled Life Bible Discovery Guide* series is designed to help you unwrap, assemble, and enjoy all God has for you in the pages of Scripture. It will focus your time and energy on the books of the Bible, the people and places they describe, and the themes and life applications that flow thick from its pages like honey oozing from a beehive.

So you can get the most out of God's Word, this series has a number of helpful features. Each study guide has no more than fourteen lessons, each arranged so you can plumb the depths or skim the surface, depending on your needs and interests.

The study guides also contain six major sections, each marked by a symbol and heading for easy identification.

    WORD WEALTH

The WORD WEALTH feature provides important definitions of key terms.

BEHIND THE SCENES

BEHIND THE SCENES supplies information about cultural beliefs and practices, doctrinal disputes, business trades, and the like, that illuminate Bible passages and teachings.

AT A GLANCE

The AT A GLANCE feature uses maps and charts to identify places and simplify themes or positions.

BIBLE EXTRA

Because this study guide focuses on a book of the Bible, you will find a BIBLE EXTRA feature that guides you into Bible dictionaries, Bible encyclopedias, and other resources that will enable you to glean more from the Bible's wealth if you want something extra.

PROBING THE DEPTHS

Another feature, PROBING THE DEPTHS, will explain controversial issues raised by particular lessons and cite Bible passages and other sources to which you can turn to help you come to your own conclusions.

FAITH ALIVE

Finally, each lesson contains a FAITH ALIVE feature. Here the focus is, So what? Given what the Bible says, what does it mean for my life? How can it impact my day-to-day needs, hurts, relationships, concerns, and whatever else is important to me? FAITH ALIVE will help you see and apply the practical relevance of God's literary gift.

As you'll see, these guides supply space for you to answer the study and life-application questions and exercises. You may, however, want to record all your answers, or just the overflow from your study or application, in a separate notebook or journal. This would be especially helpful if you think you'll dig into the BIBLE EXTRA features. Because the exercises in this feature are optional and can be expanded as far as you want to take them, we have not allowed writing space for them in this study guide. So you may want to have a notebook or journal handy for recording your discoveries while working through to this feature's riches.

The Bible study method used in this series revolves around four basic steps: observation, interpretation, correlation, and application. Observation answers the question, What does the text say? Interpretation deals with, What does the text mean?—not with what it means to you or me, but what it meant to its original readers. Correlation asks, What light do other Scripture passages shed on this text? And application, the goal of Bible study, poses the question, How should my life change in response to the Holy Spirit's teaching of this text?

If you have used a Bible much before, you know that it comes in a variety of translations and paraphrases. Although you can use any of them with profit as you work through the *Spirit-Filled Life Bible Discovery Guide* series, when Bible passages or words are cited, you will find they are from the New King James Version of the Bible. Using this translation with this series will make your study easier, but it's certainly not necessary.

The only resources you need to complete and apply these study guides are a heart and mind open to the Holy Spirit, a prayerful attitude, and a pencil and a Bible. Of course, you may draw upon other sources, such as commentaries, dictionaries, encyclopedias, atlases, and concordances, and you'll even find some optional exercises that will guide you into these sources. But these are extras, not necessities. These study guides are comprehensive enough to give you all you need to gain a good, basic understanding of the Bible book being covered and how you can apply its themes and counsel to your life.

A word of warning, though. By itself, Bible study will not transform your life. It will not give you power, peace, joy, comfort, hope, and a number of other gifts God longs for you to unwrap and enjoy. Through Bible study, you will grow in your understanding of the Lord, His kingdom and your place in it, and those things are essential. But you need more. You need to rely on the Holy Spirit to guide your study and your application of the Bible's truths. He, Jesus promised, was sent to teach us "all things" (John 14:26; cf. 1 Cor. 2:13). So as you use this series to guide you through Scripture, bathe your study time in prayer, asking the Spirit of God to illuminate the text, enlighten your mind, humble your will, and comfort your heart. He will never let you down.

My prayer and goal for you is that as you unwrap and begin to explore God's Book for living His way, the Holy Spirit will fill every fiber of your being with the joy and power God longs to give all His children. So read on. Be diligent. Stay open and submissive to Him. You will not be disappointed. He promises you!

Lesson 1/View from a Cell
(Overview and Eph. 1:1–14)

Forty years ago the jail was the nicest building in the small West Virginia town. Actually, it was the county courthouse, but to a small boy whose uncle was the sheriff the new sandstone building on the riverbank smack in the middle of town was the jail.

He didn't care about the offices and courtrooms on the main floor or the second floor. It was Saturday and they were all closed, but in the basement his uncle was at work, and in the back were the cells. He wanted to go back there and talk to the prisoner. He'd had a glimpse of him when his aunt brought lunch in a basket for her husband and then took some back to the prisoner.

Well, his aunt seemed to think that a boy had no business getting friendly with a jailbird. His uncle just shrugged. See, he thought that guy was safe, but the boy knew there was no use arguing with his aunt about really important guy stuff, like meeting your first felon.

So he had to settle for going around the corner and throwing rocks off the bridge. He kept watching the back of the jail where the whole wall of the basement was above the river level—especially the barred window of one particular cell. But the prisoner didn't look out. The boy thought that was too bad, because you could see the backs of all the buildings up and down the river. It really was a nice jail, and he thought the view from the cell was pretty good.

PAUL'S RAP SHEET

What was a nice Jewish boy, trained in Jerusalem to be a rabbi, doing in a Roman jail in the first century? Surely there had to be some mistake. But when Saul of Tarsus, leading persecutor of the fledgling Christian church, became Paul the apostle, evangelist of the Gentiles, he also became a lightning rod for Jewish anger. When Paul listed for the Corinthians all the many persecutions he had endured, one of them was frequent imprisonment (2 Cor. 11:23). He had seen the views from several cells.

There is quite a story leading up to the composition from this Roman prison of Ephesians, Philippians, Colossians, and Philemon. Read Acts 21 and identify the following aspects of the arrest of Paul.

The city where he was arrested   *Jerusalem*

The location in the city   *In the temple*

The arresting officers   *Commander of Roman cohort*

The reason the populace was upset   *Paul preached to all men against the Jews, the Law and brought Greeks into the temple*

The reason the arresting officer seized Paul

They were trying to kill Paul. He could not find out the facts because of the uproar.

If the misunderstanding surrounding the arrest of Paul had involved anything less emotionally charged to the Jewish leaders than the direct inclusion of Gentiles in the blessing of God, Paul might have soon been released with an apology. The Sadducean leadership of the Sanhedrin chose this opportunity as their chance to eliminate the man who had wreaked havoc in Jewish communities throughout Asia Minor and Greece. From Acts 22—24, describe the events that led up to Paul's initial hearing before a Roman official.

Attitude of arresting officers (22:24–29)

Ordered that Paul be scourged to find out the reason why they were shouting against Paul.

Attitude of the Jewish leaders (23:12–15)

Formed a conspiracy to kill Paul.

Protection given Paul (23:16–35)

Official to hear Paul's case (23:23–26)

Those who brought official charges against Paul (24:1)

The official charges against Paul (24:2–9)

Paul's defense against the charges (24:10–21)

The outcome of the hearing (24:22)

Paul must have been pleased to face a knowledgeable judge who would be more impressed with his Roman citizenship than with the shaky charges brought against him through a hired mouthpiece. However, Roman law did not always work efficiently or justly in the provinces far from Rome. From Acts 24 and 25, describe Paul's stay in Caesarea.

The length of his detention there (24:27)

The nature of Paul's detention in Caesarea (24:23)

The changing attitudes of Felix toward Paul (24:24–27)

When Felix was succeeded by Festus as governor of Judea, one of the items of unfinished business Festus inherited was the noncase against Paul. The Sanhedrin had not forgotten about Paul. They had been glad to have him out of circulation, but when the new governor took power, the Jewish council took the offensive again. From Acts 25 and 26, describe the conclusion of Paul's detention in Caesarea.

The Jewish strategy (25:1–4)

The attempt of Festus to untangle a knotted problem (25:5–9)

Paul's last resort to save his life (25:10–12)

The private opinion of the authorities (26:30–32)

Transporting Paul sixty miles from Jerusalem to Caesarea had been a mad dash with cavalry escort. Getting him across the fifteen hundred miles separating Caesarea from Rome was a different matter. From Acts 27 and 28, describe Paul's journey to Rome.

Means of transportation (27:1, 2)

Plan for the journey (27:1–12)

Unexpected developments (27:13—28:10)

Paul's role in emergencies (27:13—28:10)

The final leg of the journey (28:11–16)

AT A GLANCE

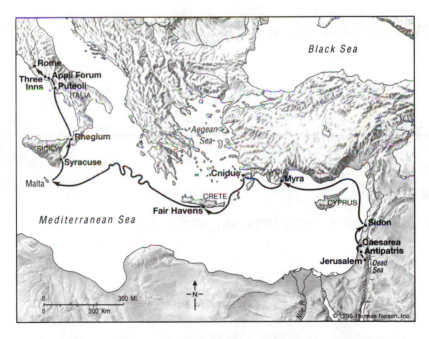

On to Rome (Paul's Fourth Journey, Acts 27:1—28:16). In Jerusalem following his third missionary journey, Paul struggled with Jews who accused him of profaning the temple (Acts 21:26–34). He was placed in Roman custody in Caesarea for two years, but after appealing to Caesar, was sent by ship to Rome. After departing the island of Crete, Paul's party was shipwrecked on Malta by a great storm. Three months later he finally arrived at the imperial city.[1]

When Paul arrived in Rome, he began immediately to explore the standing of his case. Any hopes he may have had for a speedy conclusion to a process that had already taken about two and one-half years proved groundless. From Acts 28:17–31, describe Paul's situation in Rome.

His place of detention

The length of Paul's detention

The status of the case by the Jerusalem Sanhedrin

The attitude of the Jewish community at Rome toward Paul

Paul's activities during imprisonment

FAITH ALIVE

At least four and one-half years passed from the time of Paul's arrest outside the temple in Jerusalem until he was released from imperial custody in Rome. What do you think

Paul learned about God's control of human lives during this lengthy and varied set of experiences?

Why do you think God sometimes takes us at our busiest moments and puts us in situations that force us to slow down and live at a very different pace?

PAUL'S MAILBAG

In early spring of A.D. 61 Paul arrived in Rome[2] and was detained under house arrest for two years. The New Testament contains four epistles that Paul wrote during this Roman imprisonment: Ephesians, Philippians, and Colossians were directed to churches and Philemon to an individual in the Colossian church. The letters contain clues to the nature of Paul's confinement, his spiritual life during this uncertain time, and the progress of his imperial court case.

It is possible to get the idea that Paul's house arrest was pleasant, sort of a forced vacation. How do these passages from the prison epistles fill in the grimmer side of his imprisonment? (Eph. 6:20; Phil. 1:7, 13, 14; Col. 4:18)

How did Paul keep in perspective that his imprisonment had a spiritual purpose? (Eph. 3:1, 13; 4:1; Phil. 1:12–14; Philem. 1, 9)

What was Paul's repeated prayer request of his readers? (Eph. 6:19, 20; Col. 4:3, 4)

What impact did Paul have on his captors? (Phil. 1:13; 4:22)

What was Paul's expectation about the outcome of his imprisonment? (Phil. 1:24, 25; 2:24; Philem. 22)

What were some of the lessons Paul learned or had re-inforced through his imprisonment?

Eph. 6:10–20

Phil. 1:12–18

Phil. 1:19–26

Phil. 3:7–11

Phil. 4:10–13

Col. 1:24

Philem. 10–16

Colossians and Philemon are letters yoked together by the names of people Paul mentioned in both. List below the people mentioned both in Colossians 4:7–18 and Philemon 2, 10, 23, 24.

This coincidence of people is generally accepted as evidence that Philemon lived in Colosse.

Ephesians and Colossians are also linked together by one particular person whom Paul mentioned in both. Who was he? (Eph. 6:21; Col. 4:7–9)

What task did Paul entrust to this person?

Most biblical scholars assume that this person carried the Ephesian and Colossian letters to their destinations, accompanied by Onesimus (Col. 4:9) who was delivering Paul's personal note to Philemon (Philem. 10, 17).

 ## BEHIND THE SCENES

The Influence of Paul[3]

The Philippian letter stands alone. Geographically, Philippi was in the province of Macedonia in northern Greece while Ephesus and Colosse were near one another in the province of Asia in Asia Minor. Philippians seems separated in time from the other letters within the two years of Paul's imprisonment as indicated by the tone of his expectation of release.

Compare Philippians 1:25 and 2:24 with Philemon 22. In Philemon, Paul still looks to the prayers of his fellow believers to lead to his release. In Philippians, Paul is confident his release is secured and that he can come to Philippi shortly. It would seem that Philippians was written some time after the other three letters near the end of Paul's two-year imprisonment when the case was all but decided.[4]

     FAITH ALIVE

Which of the ideas from the prison epistles that Paul learned or had reinforced by imprisonment made the greatest impression on you as you summarized them?

How would your Christian life be stronger if you applied this concept more consistently?

PAUL'S PRISON PRAISE

The Epistle to the Ephesians opens with a marvelous prayer in which Paul says, "Blessed *be* the God and Father of our Lord Jesus Christ" (1:3). In this passage of scripture Paul makes reference to what is termed the Godhead. Genesis 1:26 introduces us to this triune nature of God—or the Godhead.

The Bible clearly teaches that there is only one God (Deut. 6:4; James 2:19). Yet Genesis 1:26 introduces us to the fact that there is more than one person in the Godhead. In Genesis 1:26 and Genesis 11:7 we see the persons of the Trinity in communication with each other. The three persons of the Trinity or the Godhead are God the Father, the Son (Jesus Christ), and the Holy Spirit.

For a further understanding of the three persons of the Godhead look up Isaiah 6:8, Matthew 3:16, 17, John 1:1–3, John 16:7–14, Acts 2:38, 39, Acts 10:38, 44, 45, and Acts 13:2.

While Philippians, Colossians, and Philemon are intensely personal and obviously directed at the contemporary situations of the recipient churches, Ephesians is a more general letter that does not address particular situations or people.

Some ancient Greek manuscripts of Ephesians do not contain a place name in 1:1. There is a blank instead. Many scholars think this indicates that Ephesians was a letter written to all of the churches in the province of Asia, and that it circulated among them. If this is so, Ephesians may be the letter the Colossians were to expect to come to them from neighboring Laodicea (Col. 4:16).[5]

Ephesians 1:1, 2 opens the epistle with a three-part greeting. What functions do the parts of the greeting accomplish, and what information do they contain?

       FUNCTION   INFORMATION

1.

2.

3.

The prayer of praise in Ephesians 1:3–14 is divided into three parts by a repeated phrase in verses 6, 12, and 14. What is that phrase?

How does that repeated phrase relate to the opening line, "Blessed *be* the God and Father of our Lord Jesus Christ"? (Eph. 1:3)

Which member of the Godhead is primarily spoken of in each of the portions of this prayer?

1:3–6

1:7–12

1:13, 14

Ephesians 1:3 encompasses all of the divine activity on behalf of God's people that Paul mentioned in verses 4–14. What did Paul call all of this divine activity?

In Ephesians 1:4–6, what spiritual blessings did Paul say are ours as believers in Jesus Christ?

In Ephesians 1:7–12, what spiritual blessings did Paul say that we as believers in Jesus Christ have "in Him"?

In Ephesians 1:13, 14, what did Paul say we as believers in Jesus Christ are sealed with?

What is the "guarantee of our inheritance"?

 WORD WEALTH

Seal, *sphragis.* "In the ancient world the *seal* was the personal sign of the owner or the sender of something important, and thus, as in a letter, it distinguished what was true from what was spurious. It also was the guarantee that the thing sealed had been carried intact. . . . Here it is clearly intended that the Holy Spirit's presence is the seal. The Spirit in the believer's life is the undeniable mark of God's work in and for him. He is also the means by whom the Christian can be kept 'intact' till the day of the Lord." [6]

 WORD WEALTH

Guarantee, *arrabon.* In addition to being a "seal," the Holy Spirit is also called "the guarantee of our inheritance" (Eph. 1:14). A business term that speaks of earnest money, a part of the purchase price paid in advance as a down payment. *Arrabon* is the first installment, which guarantees full possession when the whole is paid later. *Arrabon* describes the Holy Spirit as the pledge of our future joys and bliss in heaven. The Holy Spirit gives us a foretaste or guarantee of things to come.[7]

FAITH ALIVE

Write your own personalized prayer of praise to God for what He has done in your life, using Ephesians 1:6–14 as a basis. Study the following verses and in your prayer of praise incorporate the five truths listed below as reasons to be thankful.

(v. 4) He chose us.

(v. 5) He predestined us to adoption as sons.

(v. 7) We have redemption.

(v. 11) We have obtained an inheritance.

(v. 13) We were sealed with the Holy Spirit.

1. *Spirit-Filled Life Bible* (Nashville, TN: Thomas Nelson Publishers, 1991), map on 1678.

2. Richard Longenecker, "Acts," *The Expositor's Bible Commentary*, Vol. 9 (Grand Rapids, MI: Zondervan Publishing House, 1981), 566.

3. *Spirit-Filled Life Bible,* map on 1680.

4. Everett F. Harrison, *Introduction to the New Testament* (Grand Rapids, MI: Wm. B. Eerdmans Publishing Company, 1964), 301.

5. Ibid., 310–311.

6. Francis Foulkes, *The Epistle of Paul to the Ephesians* (Grand Rapids, MI: Wm. B. Eerdmans Publishing Company, 1963), 56.

7. *Spirit-Filled Life Bible,* 1753, "Word Wealth: 1:22 guarantee."

Lesson 2/Surprised by New Life
(Eph. 1:15—2:22)

A skim of black ice mottled the streets under the silent glare of streetlights. The stillness of the January night compressed reality into the confines of their car as John and Sue hurried through empty streets to the hospital.

It was ablaze with lights, but few people moved about and fewer took note of the couple admitting to maternity. John stood in the doorway of the labor cubicle as the nurse settled Sue on her gurney. Every other little room along that corridor was empty. As hours dragged by in the labor area, reality distorted like a reflection in a fun house mirror. John knew he was tired, but it was as though nothing else had ever happened or would happen again. Existence meant sitting by his wife's bedside waiting for her next contraction and trying to be encouraging.

Then something did happen. Orderlies came to wheel Sue to the delivery room. John was turned away at the automatic doors and told to wait in the fathers' room. No one else was there, but the smell of stale cigarette smoke quickly became a taste in the back of his mouth. He went for a walk in corridors filled now with cruelly awake and cheerful early morning workers.

John looked up a friend of Sue's in the business office. Peggy took one look at John and called her husband. "Get over here, Will. Sue's about to pop, and John's a zombie."

How sensitive hospital staff are to people in crisis! John thought. *It must be a difficult skill to teach.*

Will and Peggy lived in walking distance of the hospital, so Will was soon urging institutional coffee down John's throat.

John could feel some sort of grip on time, place, and event returning when Peggy rushed up to say, "John, if you want to see your daughter before they take her to the nursery, you'd better get down to delivery. She's down by the elevators."

Will guided John through a short maze of hallways and corners to a bank of staff elevators where an incubator sat alone. A red face framed with lots of dark hair grimaced against the bright lights. Little fists rubbed against the face, and the body squirmed as though uncomfortable out in the open. She seemed to be shedding the entire outer layer of skin.

Wow! John thought. *I really am a dad. She really is my daughter.*

SURPRISING POWER

John marveled at the arrival of new life in the birth of his daughter. Paul marveled in his letter to the Ephesians about the miracle of new life at the spiritual rebirth of those who place their faith in Jesus Christ as their Savior. Paul began his description of new spiritual life with a prayer that his readers might comprehend the incredible power God exercises in making alive a spiritually dead man or woman.

What prompted Paul to pray prayers of gratitude regularly for the Ephesian believers? (Eph. 1:15, 16)

What was Paul's prayer for the spiritual insight of the Ephesians? (Eph. 1:17, 18)

        FAITH ALIVE

The Spirit of Revelation. In Ephesians 1:17–19 Paul says he prays for people to receive "the spirit of wisdom and revelation," with the dual objective of their knowing Christ and understanding God's purpose and power in their lives. Such "revelation" refers to an unveiling of our hearts that we may receive insights into the <u>way</u> God's Word is intended to work in our lives. It may be used of teaching or preaching that is especially anointed in helping people see the glory of Christ and His purpose and power for them. . . .

Wisdom and understanding, as well as sound, practical speech, recommend that today's believer both know and clearly express what is meant when he or she speaks of "revelations." The Holy Spirit does indeed give us <u>revelation</u>, as this text teaches. But such prophetic insight into the Word should never be considered as equal to the actual giving of the Holy Scriptures. As helpful as insight into God's Word may be, the finality of the <u>whole</u> of the revelation of God's Holy Word is the only sure ground for building our lives (Matt. 7:24–29).[1]

What three things did Paul want the Ephesians to know by means of their heightened spiritual perception? (Eph. 1:18, 19)

What do you think Paul meant by "the hope of His calling"? (Eph. 1:18; 4:4; Col. 1:5, 23, 27)

 BEHIND THE SCENES

A *spiritual hope* is not a wishful longing. A spiritual hope is a certainty based in the world of invisible realities that do not make impressions on the five senses. The invisible spiritual realm is not less real than the visible physical world. The invisible spiritual world includes God, angels and demons, heaven and hell, faith, hope, and love. It is a permanent world. It preceded the visible physical world and will outlast it.

Spiritual hopes are certainties. When Paul wrote, "Christ in you, the hope of glory" (Col. 1:27), he was expressing a rock-bottom reality that the eye of the spirit alone can see.

What do you think Paul meant by "the riches of the glory of His inheritance"? (Eph 1:18; see 1:11, 14; 5:5; Col. 1:12; 3:24; 1 Pet. 1:4)

What kind of power does God direct toward the lives of His children? (Eph. 1:19–21)

BEHIND THE SCENES

Principality, power, might, and *dominion* "are terms consistently used for ruling authorities in both the visible and the invisible realms (see 3:10). The New Testament reveals an invisible hierarchy of evil powers who deceive and manipulate human behavior, thereby advancing satanic strategies. Christ Himself and all who are in Christ are shown to be placed in authority above these powers, an authority that only spiritual warfare can assert, demonstrate, and sustain (6:12)."[2]

According to Ephesians 1:22, 23, who is the ultimate beneficiary of the power of God that subjects everything to the Lord Jesus Christ?

According to Ephesians 1:23, how important is the church to the Lord Jesus Christ?

 BEHIND THE SCENES

The primary thrust of this letter is to show the church as the present, physical presence of Christ. The church is to be filled with Him by the Holy Spirit, and assigned by the Lord Jesus to represent Him to society to minister His life, love, and power.[3]

 FAITH ALIVE

What is there about "the hope of His calling" (Eph. 1:18) that can encourage you in your Christian walk today?

What is there about "the riches of the glory of His inheritance" (1:18) that can change the way you relate to both problems and new opportunities?

What is there about "the exceeding greatness of His power toward us who believe" (1:19) that should inspire confidence in your daily life?

AMAZING REGENERATION

The fact that God has infinite power means that He can deal with the problem of sin. The fact that God has infinite grace and mercy means that He *wants* to deal with the problem of sin. Amazing regeneration is the story of amazing grace.

What is the greatest expression of the power of God in human experience? (Eph. 2:1)

How does this expression of power relate to the exaltation of Christ to supremacy in the spiritual world? (Compare 1:21 and 2:2.)

What are the characteristics of spiritual death? (2:3)

What attributes of God does He exercise in regenerating a sinner? (2:4, 5, 7)

 WORD WEALTH

Grace, *charis.* A characteristic of God's actions toward His children. Grace keeps company with mercy and kindness because grace is God's beneficial activity that no one deserves—"unmerited favor" it is often called.

Another dimension of grace to keep in mind is that the Greek term for "grace" is derived from the term for "joy."

God's graciousness should, in some way, involve joy.
Perhaps His graciousness gives God joy. Certainly it should
give us joy. Perhaps "grace" can be defined as God's activity
on our behalf that makes us glad.

 WORD WEALTH

Heavenly *places,* epouranious. "Does not refer to
heaven in the sense of its being the destined home of the redeemed. Rather, the Greek word here refers to the invisible
realm that surrounds our present daily situation, the arena or
sphere of spiritual action and activity. Christ's authority, which
encompasses every age and exceeds every known power, is
here and now."[4]

How do grace, faith, and good works relate to salvation?
(2:8, 9)

Compare Satan's work in "the sons of disobedience" with
God's "workmanship" in Christ Jesus. (2:3, 10)

 WORD WEALTH

Workmanship, *poiema.* Signifies that which is manufactured, a product, a design produced by an artisan. *Poiema*
emphasizes God as the Master Designer, the universe as His
creation (Rom. 1:20), and the redeemed believer as His new
creation (Eph. 2:10). Before conversion our lives had no
rhyme or reason. Conversion brought us balance, symmetry,
and order. We are God's poem, His work of art.[5]

FAITH ALIVE

What has God done for you that will enable Him to display your life as a trophy of grace in the ages to come? (Eph. 2:6, 7)

What good works do you think God has prepared for you to do in your Christian life? (2:10)

UNEXPECTED RECONCILIATION

Paul turned from developing the doctrine of regeneration to applying it to the practical problem of the relationship of Jews and Gentiles within the body of Christ. The surprising new life in Christ transcends ethnic barriers that have divided people for centuries.

What was the spiritual status of the Gentiles before Christ included them in His sacrificial death for sins? (Eph. 2:11, 12)

What is the spiritual status of believing Gentiles now that Christ has included them in His sacrificial death for sins? (2:13)

How did Christ remove the basis for spiritual animosity between Jews and Gentiles? (2:15–18)

BEHIND THE SCENES

Gentiles Embraced by Christ's Sacrifice. Prior to the New Covenant, Gentiles were excluded from citizenship in the commonwealth of Israel and were foreigners to the covenant promises of God. There was no hope in this life and no ability to know God's presence in the world. The covenant sacrifice of Christ's blood took Gentile believers who were far from God and joined them together with the Jews in the New Covenant. Gentiles were grafted in to enjoy the covenants of promise through the New Covenant and were included as heirs with the patriarchs of all of God's promises.[6]

In Ephesians 2:19–22, Paul illustrated the unity of Jewish and Gentile believers by comparing the church as a body of believers to a temple. In his comparison, what did Paul say about each of these aspects of the temple?

The foundation

The superstructure

The function

What was the role of the Holy Spirit in uniting Jews and Gentiles into a peaceful body and a holy temple? (Eph. 2:18, 22)

FAITH ALIVE

The surprising new spiritual life in Christ springs from the application of God's infinite power on behalf of sinful people. Not surprisingly, it is the grace of God that motivates this tremendous release of power through the blood of Jesus and that unites into one body of believers regenerated sinners from all kinds of backgrounds.

What diverse groups of people who normally don't get along have you seen reconciled within the relationships of the body of Christ?

What common beliefs can unite diverse people in Christ?

What common practices can unite diverse people in Christ?

At this point in your Christian experience, what do you find most surprising or remarkable about the new life God provides sinful people through His Son Jesus Christ? Why is this remarkable to you?

1. *Spirit-Filled Life Bible* (Nashville, TN: Thomas Nelson Publishers, 1991), 1788, "Kingdom Dynamics: The Spirit of Revelation."
2. Ibid., note on 1:21.
3. Ibid., note on 1:22, 23.
4. Ibid., note on 1:20.
5. Ibid., 1789, "Word Wealth: 2:10 workmanship."
6. Ibid., 1789–1790, "Kingdom Dynamics: Gentiles Embraced by Christ's Sacrifice."

Lesson 3/Surprised by Unity
(Eph. 3:1—4:16)

Rumpelstiltskin had a secret that he guarded carefully. He let no one know his name. Three times the crafty little man had spun straw into gold for the lovely miller's daughter. Then she became the queen, and a year later Rumpelstiltskin appeared to claim her firstborn child as the price for his magic. The queen could only escape his claim if she could tell him his name within three days.

The unhappy young woman guessed and guessed all the names, common and unusual, that she could think of, but Rumpelstiltskin was not one of them. This was a mystery she could never solve. Rumpelstiltskin would have to reveal his name or it would remain his secret, and the royal family would be divided.

But Rumpelstiltskin would never reveal his name. His secret was his key to troubling people and getting what he wanted. But the day before he was to claim the prince, out on the mountainside where he lived his miserly life, Rumpelstiltskin's glee got the better of him, and he danced around his hut cackling that no one could guess his name.

A spy for the queen heard the boastful little man say his name and reported the mystery of his identity to her. To Rumpelstiltskin's horror, she announced his name and kept her child. The mystery was known. The royal family was kept whole, and never again could Rumpelstiltskin cause mischief in the kingdom.

Mysterious Wisdom of God

God had a secret, too, but He didn't want to keep it to Himself. He revealed it to the apostle Paul who based his whole ministry on it. Once the people to whom Paul preached and wrote knew the secret, they understood that the family of God was united and could never be divided.

From Ephesians 3:1–7, describe Paul's relationship to the mystery of God:

His status because of the mystery

God's attribute that prompted telling the mystery

God's method of telling the mystery

Who learned the mystery

The content of the mystery

How Paul got involved with the mystery

WORD WEALTH

Dispensation, *oikonomia.* The word *dispensation* (Eph. 1:10; 3:2; Col. 1:25) refers to the manner of administration or management applied to a business or estate. In Ephesians and Colossians, Paul used the term to highlight God's application of grace through the atoning death of Christ to all believing people without distinction between Jew and Gentile.

 WORD WEALTH

Mystery, *musterion.* A *mystery,* as Paul employed the word, is an aspect of reality that human wisdom and empirical skills cannot discover. God has to reveal the truth of a *mystery.* Many things about God's Person and ways could be called mysterious, but in Paul's day the truth about equal access to the grace of God in Christ for Jews and Gentiles was unimaginable in the Jewish community to which the Father first sent His Son and the gospel. (See Eph. 1:9; 3:3, 4, 9; 6:19; Col. 1:26 , 27; 2:2; 4:3.)

From Ephesians 3:8–13, describe the theology of the mystery of God.

Paul's role in the mystery

Where the mystery expresses itself

To whom the mystery shows the wisdom of God (see 1:21)

The source of the mystery

The impact of the mystery on Christians

Paul's prayer based on the mystery

WORD WEALTH

Manifold, *polupoikilos.* Many-sided like a jewel or variegated like a flower bed overflowing with many kinds and colors of flowers. The wisdom of God is so complex that no human can take it all in. The best we can do is see the facet of His wisdom turned toward us at the moment. We can take in one aspect of His wisdom at a time, but the whole escapes our comprehension.

The wisdom of God is so overpoweringly beautiful that all we can do is proclaim its wonder and enjoy one "flower" at a time. The entire garden is too much for the senses to take in.

FAITH ALIVE

Human wisdom still creates situations in which suspicion and hatred divide people. It is still a mystery which God must declare in the church to spiritual principalities and powers that all people have equal access to Him in Christ. What are the lines of division that people use to separate themselves into groups that despise one another?

What are the most polarized groups in your community?

How can your church be involved in making known the mystery of God to these polarized groups?

AWESOME FULLNESS OF GOD

Paul was moved by thoughts of the mysterious wisdom of God to pray for the Ephesians that they might be able to comprehend the full implications of all that he had said. The awe and wonder of this prayer reflect how close to the limits of human language and understanding Paul has been in discussing God's work in Christ.

This prayer, like the one in Ephesians 1:3–14, acknowledges all three members of the Godhead.

To what member of the Godhead did Paul bow his knees? (v. 14)

By what member of the Godhead did Paul say that we as believers would be strengthened? (v. 16)

According to Paul what member of the Godhead was to dwell in our hearts by faith? (v. 17)

FAITH ALIVE

The Identity of Family Is in God (Eph. 3:14, 15). Humanly speaking, we link the identity of a husband, wife, and children to their particular family name. This, however, is only a surface identification. Family identity has a deeper root.

"Family" is a word that is rooted in God: God is <u>Father</u>— the Father of our Lord Jesus Christ. In Himself, God is a "divine family." This also expresses itself in the way that God relates to people. The Bible reveals this aspect of God's nature in rich and varied use of family imagery: God is our Father; God is Husband to His people; God is like a nurturing mother; Christ is the Bridegroom of the church.

When a man and a woman come together in marriage, God extends to them this name that in essence belongs to Him—the name of <u>family.</u> Husband, wife, and children live up to the true meaning of this name as they reflect the nature and life of the divine family in their human family.[1]

If the Ephesians were going to understand God's wisdom and mystery, what quality of God did they need to understand? (3:17–19)

What do you think Paul had in mind when he prayed that the Ephesians might be "rooted and grounded in love"? (v. 17)

Why do you think that Paul pictured the love of Christ as having "width and length and depth and height" but concluded that it "passes knowledge"? (vv. 18, 19)

From Ephesians 3:14–17, what do you think "the fullness of God" is, and how do we participate in it?

FAITH ALIVE

Spiritual Leaders Pray As Well As Teach (Eph. 3:14–21). Spiritual leaders must pray for their people as well as teach them. Paul prayed that his fellow believers might know the strength of the Spirit's reinforcement in the inner person, just as a storm-tossed ship on which he once sailed was strengthened inside by bracings and undergirded outside by cables (Acts 27:17).

Knowing that the strength of Christianity is not outward laws but inward character, Paul prayed that Christ might enter through the open door of faith, dwell in their hearts, and imprint His nature upon their minds, wills, and emotions. When Christ enters a life, He brings His life—the very soil in which we take root and blossom, the ground in which our lives are founded. Prayer begets prayer, for the believer in whom Christ's love is bringing the fullness of God will learn to ask and expect great things from Him![2]

From Ephesians 3:20, 21, analyze the conclusion of Paul's prayer in these terms:

What the church can expect from God

What God can expect from the church

FAITH ALIVE

What truths from Paul's prayer in Ephesians 3:14–21 would cause you "to be strengthened with might through His Spirit in the inner man"? (v. 16)

What spiritual concepts from the first three chapters of Ephesians have expanded your understanding of "the width and length and depth and height" of the love of God? (v. 18)

For what personal concern could you ask the other members of the body of Christ to join you in asking God "to do exceedingly abundantly above all that we ask or think"? (v. 20)

DEMANDING CHALLENGE OF GOD

Unity within the body of Christ was not just an abstract theological concept to Paul. Unity needs to express itself in the attitudes and behaviors of all Christians. How did Paul, in Ephesians 4:1–3, urge the Ephesians to express unity?

In terms of their calling as Christians

In terms of their attitudes

In terms of their relationship with the Holy Spirit

What do you think each of the following common factors
of Christian experience in Ephesians 4:4–6 should contribute
to your unity with all other believers?

One body

One Spirit

One hope of your calling

One Lord

One faith

One baptism

One God and Father of all

Paul did not want his readers to think that unity meant
uniformity. His next paragraph in Ephesians is devoted to

describing how diversity among individual Christians is as important to Christian unity as a common doctrine.

What do you think is the relationship between God's grace and the gifts Christ gives to each Christian? (Eph. 4:7)

In Ephesians 4:8, what does the quotation from Psalm 68:18 establish about the authority of Christ to distribute gifts to His followers?

How did Paul explain Christ's fulfillment of Psalm 68:18? (4:9, 10)

From Ephesians 4:11–16, describe the gift-giving activity of Christ to the church.

His gifts

The function of the gifts

The goal of the function

The measure of maturity

The risks of immaturity

The pattern of growth in the body

 FAITH ALIVE

The Gifts of the Godhead. We find Romans 12:3–8 describing gifts given by God as Father. They seem to characterize basic "motivations," that is, inherent tendencies that characterize each different person by reason of the Creator's unique workmanship in their initial gifting. . . . These gifts of our place in God's created order are foundational.

Second, in 1 Corinthians 12:7–11, the nine gifts of the Holy Spirit are listed. Their purpose is specific—to "profit" the body of the church. . . . These nine gifts are specifically available to *every* believer as the Holy Spirit distributes them (12:11). . . .

Third, the gifts which the Son of God has given are pivotal in assuring that the first two categories of gifts are applied in the body of the church. Ephesians 4:7–16 indicates the "office gifts" Christ has placed in the church along with their purpose. The ministry of these leaders is to "equip" the body by assisting each person: 1) to perceive the *place* the Creator has made him to fill, by His creative workmanship in him, and the possibilities that salvation now opens to his realization of what he was made to be; and 2) to receive the *power* of the Holy Spirit, and begin to respond to His gifts, which are given to expand each believer's capabilities *beyond* the created order and toward the redemptive dimension of ministry, for edifying the church and evangelizing the world.[3]

 FAITH ALIVE

The Lord Jesus Christ gives leaders as gifts to His body. (Notice that Ephesians 4:11 lists categories of leaders rather than abstract leadership skills.) How we receive and respond to His gifts is important to our personal growth and the growth and prosperity of our churches. Who are the leaders you consider to be the gifts of the Lord Jesus to your church, and what are their ministry functions?

LEADER   FUNCTION

How do you perceive that the leaders you listed in the previous question have equipped the members of your congregation to function as the body of Christ?

In what ways do you think your church has moved from immaturity toward maturity in recent years?

1. *Spirit-Filled Life Bible* (Nashville, TN: Thomas Nelson Publishers, 1991), 1791, "Kingdom Dynamics: The Identity of Family Is in God."

2. Ibid., "Kingdom Dynamics: Spiritual Leaders: Pray As Well As Teach."

3. Ibid., 2022–2023, "Kingdom Dynamics: Holy Spirit Gifts and Power: The Gifts of the Godhead."

Lesson 4/Surprised by Holiness
(Eph. 4:17—5:21)

Everyone has noticed that there aren't many positive television programs or movies. Is that because nobody watches positive programming? No. *The Cosby Show* was the most popular television program of the 1980s and *Home Improvement* has repeated that feat at the beginning of the '90s. People flocked to theaters to see *Chariots of Fire, Driving Miss Daisy,* and *Trip to Bountiful.*

It's difficult to write complex, believable characters who hold high moral values and who make good choices after struggling with selfish alternatives unless a writer is aiming for heavy psychological drama. Most contemporary escapist entertainment relies on crime, sexual situations, and flippancy that edges ever closer to cynicism. It's so much easier to write about.

Actors and actresses regularly express a preference for playing the roles of villains or anti-heroes because those parts are more challenging and interesting. Performers as well as writers seem to imagine that righteousness is boring, that only conformists choose to do the right thing when faced with the struggles of life. In addition, the trend is to portray "good" people as judgmental bigots in contrast to tolerant, good-hearted sinners.

Happily, in real life, when we meet a holy person, someone God has shaped in the crucible of life to respond to His Word and Spirit, we find an interesting, joyous man or woman. Never believe that holy people are dull and unimaginative or hateful and narrow-minded. Finding a real saint among ordinary people is comparable to finding a giant sequoia in a pine thicket. Yet God challenges each of us by the gentle prodding of His Holy Spirit to allow Him to make us holy people and lights in the midst of a dark age.

A New Way of Dressing

Paul first discussed holiness by comparing the prerequisite change of thinking to stripping off a dirty, worn-out suit of old clothes and donning an expensive, well-tailored suit of new clothes. Before behavior will change significantly, a person's entire outlook on life has to change.

From Ephesians 4:17–19, describe what had been wrong with the Ephesians' approach to life as unregenerate Gentiles.

Their minds

Their emotions (hearts)

Their consciences

Their actions

Word Wealth

Futility, *mataiotes.* The unregenerate mind is characterized by *futility.* The Greek term is similar in meaning to the

Hebrew term in Ecclesiastes which appears in the phrase
"vanity of vanities, all is vanity" (Eccl. 1:2; 12:8). The basic
meaning of both terms is "emptiness." Paul was saying that
the mind of a person apart from Christ's salvation is void of
the capacity to perceive and reason about the matters of the
unseen spiritual world. "Five traits of a worldly walk are
summed up in the word *futility* (emptiness, purposelessness):
darkened understanding, alienation from God, ignorance of
God's way, a hardened heart, and an unfeeling state."[1]

Why is everything in Ephesians 4:17–19 inconsistent with
the knowledge of Christ? (Eph. 4:20, 21)

What is being discarded when the old clothes of the old
man are stripped off? (v. 22)

What is it that has corrupted the behavior of the old man?
(v. 22)

What is there about personal desires and cravings that can
deceive and distort one's way of looking at reality to the point
that one's thinking becomes futile? (v. 22; see also vv. 17–19)

The old man is to be put off in the conduct sphere of life
(v. 22). What sphere of life does the new man involve? (v. 23)

Of the two actions—putting off the old man and putting on the new man (vv. 22, 24)—which is active, that is, something I do for myself?

Which action is passive, that is, something God must do for me through His Holy Spirit?

What makes the new man so effective in perceiving reality and carrying out the will of God? (v. 24)

BEHIND THE SCENES

The old man and the new man are not to be understood as personalities that are exchanged in the process of sanctification. The old man and the new man are favorite expressions of Paul for two ways of thinking and behaving (see Rom. 6:4, 6; Col. 3:9, 10). The old man and the new man "contrasts the old life-style dominated by the spirit of disobedience (2:1–3) with the believer's newly created capacity for a life-style of obedience by the Holy Spirit's power (2:10; 3:16)."[2]

FAITH ALIVE

The verbs "put off" and "put on" are in forms that suggest decisive actions rather than ongoing processes. Through Paul the Holy Spirit commanded the Ephesian Christians and every generation of believers since to change their spiritual clothes.

How have you experienced the deceitful, tricky nature of your desires in relation to other people, to habits, to possessions, and so on?

What patterns of thought has the Holy Spirit transformed in your life since you became a Christian?

A NEW WAY OF TALKING

If Paul surprised you by basing holiness on a renewed mind, he may startle you further by emphasizing speech above other behaviors as one that the Holy Spirit must control. What is the first characteristic of holy speech commanded in Ephesians? (4:25) What reason is given for this command? (v. 25)

In Ephesians 4:25, Paul quoted Zechariah 8:16 as a biblical basis for his teaching. Read through the eighth chapter of Zechariah which refers to the future reign of the Lord over His people. How important to the future reign of the Lord is truthful speech among His people?

After dishonesty, what is the next threat to holy speech that Paul identified? (vv. 26, 27)

In Ephesians 4:26, Paul quoted Psalm 4:4, which David the psalmist addressed to the "sons of men" (v. 2) who wished to harm him. Look up Psalm 4:4, which is a call to these enemies to repent of their wicked plans. What did David advise his opponents to do in order to prevent anger from issuing in sinful actions?

In keeping with Psalm 4:4, what would Paul expect a Christian to do before sunset to keep his anger from producing sinful words? (v. 26)

How does harboring anger and turning it into sinful words "give place to the devil"? (v. 27)

BEHIND THE SCENES

"The Greek word for place *(topos)* emphasizes that believers can actually give ground in their lives to satanic control. This is a warning against theologized suppositions that argue against the possibility that demonic vexing or oppression may succeed with Christians. But the surrounding commands balance the issue (v. 17—5:14), making clear that responsible believers cannot glibly blame the Devil for sin they yield to in carnal disobedience."[3]

In Ephesians 4:28 Paul momentarily left the subject of speech to mention stealing. Why would lying speech and angry speech remind Paul of theft? What do dishonesty and anger steal from the people involved?

What do thieves lie about and what are they angry about?

According to Paul, what is the cure for stealing? (v. 28)

Why do you think Paul demanded charitable giving beyond working for his own need as proof that the thief is transformed? (v. 28)

In Ephesians 4:29 how does the movement from "corrupt speech" (speech that tears people down) to edifying speech parallel the movement in verse 28 from stealing to charitable giving?

How does Ephesians 4:31, 32 follow the same logical pattern as verses 28 and 29?

WORD WEALTH

The words for hostile speech in Ephesians 4:31 appear to follow a progression from a sinful, but private, attitude to very public and nasty words. *Malice* is the foundational problem, a general feeling of ill will toward someone. Malice hardens into *bitterness,* a resentment of everything the other person does. Bitterness leads to *wrath,* outbursts of temper. Wrath becomes *anger,* a permanent state of emotional agitation. Anger can't help but boil over into *clamor,* occasional loud quarrels, and clamor will spread to habitual *evil speaking.* How ugly this progression of hateful attitudes and actions is, and yet how easily we slip into it. No wonder it grieves the Holy Spirit to witness such an offense against holiness.

Why does the Holy Spirit seal believers in Christ? (Eph. 4:30; see 1:13, 14)

How is sinful speech a violation of the purpose of a Christian's sealing by the Holy Spirit?

How do you think the sinful speech referred to in Ephesians 4:25–32 grieves the character of the Holy Spirit?

FAITH ALIVE

The apostle James observed, "If anyone does not stumble in word, he *is* a perfect man, able also to bridle the whole body" (James 3:2). In his letter to the Ephesians, Paul expressed the same truth.

With what aspect of speech do you have the most trouble in obeying the teaching of the Lord in Ephesians 4:25–32?

Give an example of when your speech offended the Spirit of God who dwells within you.

What change would you like the Lord to make in your pattern of speech in the immediate future for His glory and your sanctification?

A NEW WAY OF WALKING

After considering at length holiness in thinking and speech, Paul turned his attention in Ephesians to matters that we more typically associate with holiness: morality, separation from the world, and the will of God. Even in this section it's interesting how often the matter of speech intrudes.

Ephesians 5:1, 2 makes a transition from the material discussed in chapter 4. What activity of the Father are we as His children to imitate? (4:32; 5:1)

The New Testament often compares daily life to walking. In what ways is walking a good metaphor for our way of living? (5:2, 8, 15)

From Ephesians 5:2–7, explain what each of these has to do with walking in love.

Imitating Christ

Rejecting immorality

Rejecting vulgar speech

In terms of contemporary experience, what do you think is the meaning of each kind of bad speech in Ephesians 5:4 that needs to be replaced with thanksgiving?

Filthiness

Foolish talking

Coarse jesting

If these kinds of sinful speech need to be replaced with thanksgiving, they must be forms of ingratitude. How are these forms of vulgarity evidences of lack of gratitude to God?

How does Ephesians 5:7 sum up verses 3–6?

From Ephesians 5:8–14, explain what you think Paul meant by walking as "children of light."

From Ephesians 5:15–21, explain what you think each of these topics has to do with walking wisely.

Redeeming the time

Understanding the will of God

Being filled with the Spirit

Speaking to and encouraging one another in praise

Giving thanks

Submitting to one another

 FAITH ALIVE

Encouraging One Another in Praise [Ephesians 5:18, 19]. This text instructs interaction in our praise. Paul tells the Ephesians to "[speak] to one another," using psalms and hymns and spiritual songs. Entering a gathering of believers, even with a small offering of praise, our worship begins to be magnified as we join with others. Their voices encourage us, and we inspire them. Separation from the local assembly deprives a person of this relationship and its strength. Let us assemble <u>often</u> and praise much—encouraging one another in praise.[4]

 FAITH ALIVE

The old man would naturally choose to walk in hatred, darkness, and folly. The new man, with a mind renewed by God's Spirit, supernaturally chooses to walk in love, light, and wisdom.

How has God helped you to see the vulgarity of the world as an offense against His love?

How has God helped you to wake up to the shameful-
ness of the dark deeds that once did not offend you?

In what area of life do you think the Lord has given you
the most wisdom? How does that wisdom express itself?

1. *Spirit-Filled Life Bible* (Nashville, TN: Thomas Nelson Publishers, 1991), 1793, note
on 4:17–19.
2. Ibid., note on 4:22, 24.
3. Ibid., note on 4:27.
4. Ibid., 1794–1795, "Kingdom Dynamics: Encouraging One Another in Praise."

Lesson 5/Surprised by Power
(Eph. 5:22—6:24)

In the great movie *Chariots of Fire,* produced by David Putnam, the Christian athlete, Eric Liddel, learns that God's power is fully released in the life of a man who is completely submitted to Jesus Christ. While the other athletes serve gods of Olympic gold, fortune, and fame, Eric Liddel serves Jesus Christ and runs the race, not on his own strength, but by relying on God's strength.

In the film, Eric Liddel's commitment to Jesus Christ is tested many times, including the pivotal point in his running career when he must choose not to run an important race on Sunday because it is his day of worship. Yet God honors Eric's submission to Him and Eric finds incredible strength when the other athletes are broken and weary.

Eric Liddel understood that his real ability and strength did not come from mere human will, but rather a yielding to Jesus Christ. In fact, Eric knew firsthand the truth in 2 Corinthians 12:9 where the apostle Paul says, "My strength is made perfect in weakness."

The power of God is surprising, not because it exists but because of how it operates in human experience. The wisdom of the world foolishly looks for buttons to push to turn on God's power—prayers to say as though they were incantations, rules to keep so God has to fulfill His side of the bargain, and services rendered to buy His favor. But God's power is part of a Father's love for His children, an "allowance" for daily living for every believer who maintains his relationship with his heavenly Father.

STALWART SUBMISSION

Divine power is only available to Christians who approach life with an appreciation and acceptance of divine authority. The most fundamental expression of divine authority is the pattern of human relationships God established in family units. "Submitting is taking the divinely ordered place in a relationship. Submission can never be required by one human being of another; it can only be given on the basis of trust, that is, to believe God's Word and to be willing to learn to grow in relationships."[1]

From Ephesians 5:22–24, describe the instruction the Lord gives wives with regard to their husbands.

The commanded attitude

The model for this attitude

The extent of this attitude

The analogy for a wife's relationship to her husband

A synonymous term for this attitude (v. 33)

WORD WEALTH

Submit, *hupotasso.* The verb *to submit* translates a Greek term with a military background. To submit is to accept the authority structure in which you are placed. Submission involves subordinating personal interests for the well-being of the larger unit.

In the military arena, a soldier operates in a hierarchical system of rank that depends on unquestioned obedience to the commands of a superior officer. In a marriage and family, members operate in a climate of love and mutual support characterized by the way Christ and the church interact. Finding one's place in the system and working for the success of the larger unit guides the very different actions of both the soldier and the wife, husband, or child.

From Ephesians 5:26–33, describe the instruction the Lord gives husbands with regard to their wives.

The commanded attitude

The model for this attitude

The extent of this attitude

The analogy for a husband's relationship to his wife

What does the quotation of Genesis 2:24 by Paul suggest? (Eph. 5:31)

About the relationship of Christ to His church (v. 32)

About the relationship of a husband to his wife

BEHIND THE SCENES

The Bible does not put males over females, but it does call for husbands to accept responsible leadership in the same spirit of self-giving and devotion Christ has shown for His church. Women are never made second to men in general, but the wife is specifically called to accept her husband's leadership. These verses put such demands upon the Christian husband that it is impossible to see how a charge of male chauvinism could justly be made against the Bible, or how a license to exploit women or wives could ever be claimed from such texts.[2]

FAITH ALIVE

"Submitting to one another in the fear of God" (Eph. 5:21) is the concluding virtue in the walk of holiness (vv. 15–21). Ephesians 5:22–33 expands the concept of mutual submission within marriage. Answer the following questions that apply to you.

If you are a woman, married or unmarried, what do you think are the benefits of submission to a husband who loves his wife according to the pattern of Ephesians 5:25–33?

What do you think are the problems of trying to submit to a husband who mistreats and takes advantage of his wife?

If you are a man, married or unmarried, what do you think are the benefits of trying to love and aid in the growth of a wife who accepts the leadership of her husband?

What do you think are the problems of trying to love and aid in the growth of a wife who ignores the leadership of her husband?

Since the Lord does not command husbands to demand respect or wives to demand love, how can wives and husbands without nagging and sulking encourage their spouses to respond to the Lord's instruction?

How do you think marriages that reflect God's pattern for relationships between partners are strong with God's power against worldly forces that would destroy them?

OVERWHELMING OBEDIENCE

Some authority relationships depend on obedience. As with submission relationships, obedience relationships are channels through which divine power can flow into and through human lives.

From Ephesians 6:1–3, describe the instruction the Lord gives children with regard to their parents.

The commanded attitude

The motivation for the attitude

The relationship between obedience and honoring

The meaning of the promise associated with the fifth commandment

From Ephesians 6:4, describe the instruction the Lord gave fathers with regard to children.

Negatively

Positively

How does the success or failure of parents, especially fathers, in fulfilling their duties outlined in Ephesians 6:4 relate to children's carrying out of their responsibility outlined in Ephesians 6:1–3?

 FAITH ALIVE

Training and *admonition* are two nouns that complement one another as terms of child discipline. Training tends to involve all of the action-oriented methods of discipline, and

admonition tends to denote all of the verbal forms of discipline. Together training and admonition encompass all that parents do and say to prepare their children for life. It is of paramount importance that all child rearing, verbal and non-verbal, be "of the Lord," rooted in the Word of God and aimed at living for Him.

 ## FAITH ALIVE

Parents Responsible to Raise Children (Eph. 6:4). God holds parents responsible for the upbringing of children—not grandparents, not schools, not the state, not youth groups, not peers and friends. Although each of these groups may influence children, the final duty rests with parents, and particularly with the father, whom God has appointed "head" to lead and serve the family.

Two things are necessary for the proper teaching of children: a right *attitude* and a right *foundation.* An atmosphere reeking with destructive criticism, condemnation, unrealistic expectations, sarcasm, intimidation, and fear will "provoke a child to wrath." In such an atmosphere, no sound teaching can take place.

The positive alternative would be an atmosphere rich in encouragement, tenderness, patience, listening, affection, and love. In such an atmosphere parents can build into the lives of their children the precious foundation of knowledge of God.[3]

From Ephesians 6:5–8, describe the instruction the Lord gave servants with regard to masters.

The attitude

The motivation of the attitude

The ultimate reward for this attitude

What does Ephesians 6:5–7 imply are attitudes and behaviors that displease God on the part of those working for bosses?

From Ephesians 6:9, describe the instruction the Lord gave masters with regard to their servants.

"The same things" to do to servants

That which is to be given up

That which God models for masters

What does Ephesians 6:9 imply are attitudes and actions that displease God on the part of those who command workers?

FAITH ALIVE

How has your life benefited from the obedience and honor you gave (give) your parents?

What concept about parenting in Ephesians 6:4 impressed you most? Why?

Paul's instructions to slaves and masters have to be applied cautiously to employees and employers in contemporary society. The way we treat superiors or subordinates in the workplace and the way we approach our work responsibilities are two possible areas of application.

In obedience to Ephesians 6:5–9, how can you approach the people you work with in a more godly manner?

In obedience to Ephesians 6:5–9, how can you approach your work responsibilities in a more godly manner?

How do you think that Christian obedience within proper authority relationships can channel the power of God into the lives of people who observe and notice it?

AWESOME ARMAMENTS

In Ephesians 6:10–18, Paul wrote directly about the power of God that expresses itself indirectly through stalwart submission and overwhelming obedience. He compared the virtues that God produces in a Christian's life by His Holy Spirit to the pieces of armor worn at the time by a Roman legionnaire.

The power of God is not resident in the pieces of armor. Where is the power? (Eph. 6:10)

What is the function of the armor of God? (vv. 11–13)

In each of the following passages in Ephesians, what does God say He has demonstrated emphatically to the demonic forces in all of their ordered fiendishness?

1:19–21

3:8–12

6:11–13

FAITH ALIVE

"We Do Not Wrestle Against Flesh and Blood" (Eph. 6:12). One of the church's greatest demands is to discern between the spiritual struggle and other social, personal, and political difficulties. Otherwise, individual believers and groups become too easily detoured, "wrestling" with human adversaries instead of prayerfully warring against the invisible works of hell behind the scenes.

"Heavenly *places"* recalls earlier references to: 1) spiritual resources available to the church (1:3); 2) Christ's authority over evil (1:21); 3) the church's being seated together with her ascended Lord (2:6); 4) the Father's will to display His wisdom through the church to the confounding of evil powers (3:10). On these grounds the passage announces the church's corporate assignment to prayer warfare, in order that evil will be driven back and the will of God advanced.[4]

From Ephesians 6:14–17, complete the chart below about the armor of God.

PIECE OF ARMOR   CORRESPONDING SPIRITUAL COMPONENT

1.

2.

3.

4.

5.

6.

What spiritual discipline activates the armor in standing against the Devil? (Eph. 6:18)

Whose armor do your prayers activate? (v. 18)

What does this suggest about your need of the prayers of other believers?

How did Paul relate himself in a Roman prison to the spiritual warfare of the distant Ephesians? (vv. 19, 20)

FAITH ALIVE

Spiritual Warfare (Eph. 6:13–17). "The military metaphor is intended to show the reader that we are engaged in an active battle now. Though some suggest that the viewpoint of a continuous aggressive struggle minimizes the accomplished victory of the Cross, it in fact asserts the victory all the more. All spiritual warfare waged today is victorious only on the basis of appropriating the provision of the Cross and Christ's blood (Col. 2:15). 1) Personal faith that positions itself against evil and 2) aggressive prayer warfare that assails demonic strongholds are two distinct and complementary facets of spiritual life.

"This entire passage lends further support to this perspective: 'To stand against' (v. 11) means to hold at bay aggressively or to stand in front of and oppose; 'wrestle' (v. 12) means to engage actively in one-on-one combat; 'to stand' (v. 13) means to be found standing after an active battle; and 'stand' (v. 14) means take your stand for the next battle."[5]

What was the mission of Tychicus to the Ephesians? (6:21, 22)

What did Paul have to say in his salutation about each of these qualities? (6:23, 24; see 1:2)

Peace

Love

Faith

Grace

FAITH ALIVE

Paul began the Ephesian epistle with a prayer of praise for God's eternal purposes and he ended it with a call to believers to stand firm in God's great power while His purposes are being accomplished.

What do you think is the strongest piece of your spiritual armor? Why?

What do you think is the weakest piece of your spiritual armor? Why?

What can you do to strengthen this weak piece of armor?

For whom should you pray regularly as a part of your spiritual warfare?

Whom should you ask to be praying regularly for you as part of their spiritual warfare?

1. *Spirit-Filled Life Bible* (Nashville, TN: Thomas Nelson Publishers, 1991), 1795, note on 5:21, 22.

2. Ibid., notes on 5:22, 23, 24–33.

3. Ibid., 1796, "Kingdom Dynamics: Parents Responsible to Raise Children."

4. Ibid., note on 6:12.

5. Ibid., note on 6:13–17.

Lesson 6/Joy in the Gospel
(Phil. 1:1–30)

"Ram Sharan Nepal [is] a 33-year-old Nepalese pastor. With his wife, Meena, Ram provides a home and education to over 150 orphans. He is also a pastor, a Bible-school teacher, the supervisor of 96 churches, and the director of a vocational training program for Nepal's poorest citizens. . . .

"The poverty of Nepal, the world's only Hindu kingdom, is reinforced by a rigid caste system. Of the country's 20 million citizens, 5 million are 'untouchables'—shoemakers, tailors, street sweepers, toolmakers, and garbage collectors belonging to the lowest Hindu caste. Despite laws against caste discrimination, untouchables are locked at birth into a cycle of misery with no parallel in the Western world. . . .

"It was in this closed society that, at the age of 15, Ram Sharan Nepal became a follower of Jesus. The son of a Hindu farmer from northwest Nepal, Ram spent his childhood tending goats and rising early to offer sacrifices to Hindu deities.

" 'I saw firsthand the way religious leaders were robbing poor people,' recalls Ram. 'For me, Hinduism was an "outside" religion. I was looking for a religion of the heart.'

"Ram was introduced to Christianity by a classmate, the son of a pastor from Finland. 'I was drawn by the simple message of Jesus,' remembers Ram. 'Christianity was about grace, not sacrifice. It gave me a way to help people.'

"Shortly after his conversion, Ram's brother tried to kill him. Ram fled his family's home and moved to Kathmandu, the capital of Nepal. Living alone and working full-time, he found spiritual and emotional support in a small underground church of teenagers. By the age of 17, Ram was a pastor, praying for the sick and discreetly visiting new converts.

" 'We were like the church in the Book of Acts,' remembers Ram. 'We were the first generation of Christians in Nepal, and we treated one another with love and care.' . . .

"Meanwhile, social revolution was sweeping Nepal, and Ram and Meena's house church grew rapidly. Its members were largely young professionals, willing to risk imprisonment to practice a new, more democratic religion. Ram himself was frequently arrested. On one occasion he was jailed and beaten for two weeks."[1]

EXCITED ABOUT MY COMRADES

Fifteen years ago, Ram Sharan Nepal valued his Christian fellow workers above all other earthly things. Only they understood him and cared for him in a society hostile to the faith in Christ that shaped his life. Nearly two thousand years ago, Paul felt the same in a Roman prison about his Christian friends at Philippi who occupied a special place of endearment in his heart.

Compare the greetings (the first two or three verses) of Ephesians, Philippians, Colossians, and Philemon. How are they similar and different in these categories?

Senders

Receivers

Initial prayer

BEHIND THE SCENES

"Because of his close relationship with the Philippian Christians, Paul does not need to insist upon his authority as an apostle as he does in other epistles.

"*Bishops:* A reference to an official in the local church, stressing the nature of his work as an overseer. In the New Testament the word refers to the same office as elder, which emphasizes the status of the office, and pastor, which describes the shepherding function of the office."[2]

"*Deacons:* The New Testament does not define the exact nature and duties of the office of deacon, but the meaning of the word suggests the function of serving as an attendant [1 Tim 3:10]. The office probably originated with the choosing of the seven assistants to the apostles (Acts 6), but they are not referred to as such officeholders." [3]

From Philippians 1:3–8, describe the thankfulness of Paul for the Philippians.

What he was thankful for

Attitude behind his thanksgiving

What he was confident of

Why he was confident

How much he missed them

FAITH ALIVE

Key Lessons in Faith (Phil. 1:6). Our inheritance as believers can only be received fully by taking a stand on what God has said in the face of contradictory circumstances, sometimes even suffering and death. The stance of faith eliminates fear and worry and brings the freedom to "rejoice evermore." [Believe that God always finishes what he starts, including His work in you!] True faith never says, "I cannot!" Such an utterance betrays unbelief.[4]

Describe the prayer of Paul for the Philippians in Philippians 1:9–11.

About their love

About their discernment

About their interpersonal relations

About their character

    FAITH ALIVE

Paul took great delight in the Christians of Macedonia as revealed by the warm tone of the epistles to the Thessalonians and the Philippians. We all need a group of fellow believers for whom we can feel genuine love and with whom we can share a sense of mission.

For what group or individuals in your church, former church, neighborhood Bible study group, or outreach group do you feel the kind of intimacy that Paul expressed for the Philippians?

What shared experiences and beliefs created that sense of intimacy?

How should you pray for these people that they might prosper spiritually?

How should you encourage these people by sharing what God has done for you through them?

EXCITED ABOUT THE OUTCOME

Paul knew that the Philippians had tender feelings for him as well. He was concerned that they might be unduly worried about his imprisonment, so he shared with them the joy he was experiencing because of the results of his sufferings.

How did Paul, in Philippians 1:12–14, say the gospel had been furthered by his imprisonment?

In pagan Rome (see 4:22)

In the Roman church

From what two motivations was the gospel being preached in Rome? (vv. 15–17)

 WORD WEALTH

Selfish ambition, *eritheia.* Translates a Greek term that once had a honorable meaning but that has come to have a dishonorable one. Originally, this term referred to a field-worker or reaper, and later anyone working for pay, a hireling. In the course of time and usage, this noun came to describe a person who was concerned only with his own welfare, a person susceptible to being bribed, an ambitious, self-willed person seeking opportunities for promotion. From there it became electioneering, a partisan factious spirit that would resort to any method for winning followers.[5]

Why do you think some Christians in Rome might have wanted to make Paul unhappy, and how do you think they might have reckoned that proclaiming the gospel with selfish motives would have distressed him?

How did Paul react to this mixture of good and bad motives for proclaiming the gospel? (Phil. 1:18)

BEHIND THE SCENES

"Rather than slowing the spread of the gospel, Paul's imprisonment has given him new opportunities for witnessing, particularly among the elite of the Roman army. His experience has also stimulated others to preach more boldly, even though some have the wrong motive. Paul has no scathing remark for these people because their doctrine is correct. His reaction is vastly different to the doctrinal agitators addressed in chapter 3." [6]

FAITH ALIVE

One danger of living in a society saturated with churches and parachurch ministries is losing a sense of urgency about evangelizing the lost. It's easy to assume that someone else will proclaim the gospel even if we never do.

When was the most recent time that you experienced emotion you could call joy because the gospel had been proclaimed?

What was there about that gospel situation that caused you joy?

How can you help promote a spirit of cooperation and support rather than competition and criticism among the churches and groups in your community that proclaim the gospel, even though they have differing doctrinal positions and church practices?

Ask the Lord to guide you in setting an evangelistic target for your own witness and the witness of your church for the rest of this year. Write these targets in the space below and pray regularly that the Lord would give you joy in seeing these targets reached.

EXCITED ABOUT MY OPTIONS

Paul's confinement in Rome seemed to give him sharper perspectives on time and eternity. He was pleased to share with the Philippians the peace God had given him about his future.

Paul knew that his rejoicing in the bold witnessing by the Roman Christians would lead to deliverance, that is, spiritual victory, because of the faithfulness of the Philippians and Jesus Christ. What was Paul counting on from each of these sources? (Phil. 1:19)

The Philippians

Jesus Christ

What was Paul's "earnest expectation and hope"? (1:20)

Negatively

Positively

What did Paul mean when he said, "For to me, to live *is* Christ"? (vv. 21–24; see Gal. 2:20)

What did Paul mean when he said, "For to me . . . to die *is* gain"? (vv. 21–24)

Which option was Paul confident he would be exercising? (vv. 24–26)

What sort of celebration did Paul want when he was restored to the Philippians from his Roman imprisonment? (v. 26; see v. 20)

 FAITH ALIVE

Paul rejoiced in anticipation of service for Christ in life or enjoyment of Christ after death. Personally he preferred the presence of his Lord, but faithfully he recognized the need for his ministry to continue.

Reflect on the idea of being in the presence of Christ in glory. What aspects of that awesome prospect appeal to you and give you joy?

What aspects of your family, ministry, civic, career, and other involvements are significant reasons to want to continue serving God in this life?

EXCITED ABOUT YOUR OBEDIENCE

Paul concluded the first chapter of Philippians by appealing to the church to make his joy greater by persevering to the end. They had served faithfully with Paul in the spread of the gospel, and he wanted them to continue to live lives worthy of the gospel.

According to Philippians 1:27, 28, what standard did Paul desire to characterize the conduct of the Philippians?

Their reputation

Their unity

Their approach to adversity

BEHIND THE SCENES

"Conduct: This word usually describes one's life as a citizen. The city of Philippi prized its Roman citizenship, but Paul reminds his readers that the most important conduct is to behave in a manner befitting citizens of the kingdom of God." [7]

According to Philippians 1:29, what two activities are Christians asked to engage in on Christ's behalf?

1.

2.

WORD WEALTH

"To you it has been granted on behalf of Christ. . . to suffer for His sake" (Phil. 1:29). The verb "to grant" derives from the noun for "grace." Paul regarded both faith in Christ and suffering for Christ as divine favors. Suffering is never fun, nor should it be masochistically looked for. When God permits it, however, we should expect great things from Him in terms of character development in our lives and spiritual impact on the lives of others.

FAITH ALIVE

In spite of imprisonment, Paul knew great joy. His anticipation of obedience by the Philippians to his instruction to bravely face the same kind of persecution he had faced cheered his spirits.

Why do you think opponents of Christians think we should be afraid of them?

Why shouldn't we be afraid of them?

What has God taught you through persecution or ridicule by unbelievers?

In what ways do you think the Lord Jesus might expect Christians to suffer persecution in our culture and society?

1. Barbara R. Thompson, "Nepal's Book of Acts," *Christianity Today* (November 9, 1992), 15–17.
2. *Spirit-Filled Life Bible* (Nashville, TN: Thomas Nelson Publishers, 1991), 1802, note on 1:1.
3. Ibid., 1844, note on 3:8.
4. Ibid., "Truth-in-Action through Philippians: 1808–1809, Key Lessons in Faith."
5. Ibid., 1802, "Word Wealth: 1:16 selfish ambition."
6. Ibid., note on 1:12–18.
7. Ibid., 1803, note on 1:27.

Lesson 7/Joy in Jesus: Humility
(Phil. 2:1–30)

"Pride grows in the human heart like lard on a pig," observed Aleksandr Solzhenitsyn after his imprisonment in the old Soviet gulag.[1] "The line dividing good and evil cuts through the heart of every human being. And who is willing to destroy a piece of his own heart?" he added. "During the life of any heart this line keeps changing places; sometimes it is squeezed one way by exuberant evil and sometimes it shifts to allow enough space for good to flourish."[2]

Solzhenitsyn learned in the prison camps that everything we pride ourselves in can be taken away: possessions, social position, physical attractiveness, power over people, security, and so on. These things attach themselves to the fat on the evil side of the heart. For the prisoners who prided themselves in what they had, too much of their hearts were cut away when these things were taken, and they could not survive the camps.

The men or women who let go of all the trappings of pride and clung to Christ in the inner sanctuary of their souls were impervious to the dog-eat-dog society of the prisoners and the brutality of the penal authorities. The humility of Jesus made their hearts pure and strong, shining glimpses of Christ Himself in a dark spiritual wasteland.

REJOICE IN LOWLINESS

The glitzy, soul-numbing materialism of the western world may not pose much threat to life and limb, but it threatens the human spirit as certainly as the Soviet prison camps.

Paul saw a similar threat in the culture of the first century. He prescribed the humility of Jesus as the medicine for a heart fat and sick with pride.

On what three bases did Paul appeal to the Philippians to regard one another without favoritism? (2:1) What do you think he meant by each of these expressions?

BASIS FOR UNITY   MEANING

1.

2.

3.

In what four ways did Paul say the Philippians could make him joyous by showing that they did not play favorites among themselves? (2:2)

1.

2.

3.

4.

How did Paul say that humility is motivated in treating other people? (2:3, 4)

Negatively

Positively

From Philippians 2:5–8, describe how Paul used the example of Jesus to teach the Philippians to be humble servants.

Paul's goal for the Philippians

Jesus' starting point

Jesus' attitude

Jesus' first step of humility

Jesus' second step of humility

What should the Philippians have concluded about Christian humility from the example of Jesus? (vv. 5–8)

WORD WEALTH

Made Himself of no reputation, *kenoo.* "The reality of the Incarnation is expressed in the complete self-renunciation of Christ as He 'made Himself of no reputation' (emptied Himself of His privileges). He veiled the manifestations of deity and assumed real humanity. 'Likeness' suggests that Jesus was really a man. His humanity was genuine, yet His being was still divine."[3]

According to Philippians 2:9–11, what have been the results of the voluntary humiliation of Jesus?

From God

From created beings

What should the Philippians have concluded are the spiritual results of voluntary humility on the part of followers of Jesus? (vv. 9–11)

![FAITH ALIVE icon] **FAITH ALIVE**

Faith Exalting Jesus' Lordship (Phil. 2:9–11). Scholars note that the word *confess* means "to acknowledge openly and joyfully, to celebrate and give praise" (Thayer/Wycliffe). This eloquently and beautifully stated text is a great point of acknowledgement for all who would learn the power of faith's confession. The exalting and honoring of our Lord Jesus Christ is our fountainhead of power in applying faith.

The Father honors Him first, then those who confess His Son as well (John 12:26). All humans, angels, and demon spirits will ultimately bow the knee to Jesus, rendering complete and final homage. That confession of every tongue will one day be heard by every ear as He receives ultimate and complete rule.

But until that day, our confession of Jesus Christ as Lord invites and receives His presence and power over all evil whenever we face it now. And as we declare His lordship—in faith—His rule enters those settings and circumstances today.[4]

 ### FAITH ALIVE

The incarnation of Jesus does not save people; the atoning death of Jesus as a sacrifice for sins is His saving work. The Incarnation, however, provides many valuable lessons for redeemed men and women about how to live for Jesus. Choosing the path of humble service is a major lesson of the Incarnation.

How can you esteem or value others as better than yourself (Phil. 2:3) when you have greater intelligence or talent than they do or when you don't like them?

What sorts of tasks in the church does pride want you to think are beneath your dignity?

What does the example of Jesus suggest to you is the measure of how highly the Father will exalt you in His kingdom?

What opportunities to serve the Lord and people are available to you right now?

Devote some prayer time to asking for direction about whether to accept one or more of those service opportunities.

REJOICE IN OBEDIENCE

Humble people are serving people. Paul followed his lesson about joyful humility with one about joyful obedience to the work and will of God.

From Philippians 2:12, 13, describe the human and divine aspects of the outworking of salvation by grace through faith.

Human aspect

Divine aspect

    BEHIND THE SCENES

"In view of the obedience of Christ and His lordship [Phil. 2:5–11], the Philippians should show a like obedience [v. 12]. Paul does not teach that salvation is dependent on one's continued works, but that salvation must express itself in progressive Christian living and upright character, not only individually, but through obedient participation in God's corporate call to a local church."[5]

From Philippians 2:14–16, describe the characteristics of joyous obedience that Paul commanded of the Philippians.

In words

In reputation

In contrast to the world

In witness

In encouraging leaders

 WORD WEALTH

The world is spiritually "crooked and perverse" (Phil. 2:15). The adjective *crooked* simply describes unbelievers as spiritually out of alignment with the truth of God. *Perverse* adds the active notion that unbelievers are spiritually twisted or distorted by Satan who opposed the truth of God and convinced the world of a lie. Believers are to abhor evil (Rom. 12:9) because it is a freakish, twisted approach to life that offends the Creator and harms His creatures.

Read Numbers 15:1–10 where Moses instructed the Israelites about giving thanks to God by pouring a drink offering of wine over burnt offerings of various sorts. In Philippians 2:17 (see 1:20, 21), how did Paul apply the concept of a burnt offering and a drink offering to himself and the Philippians?

How could Paul consider the possibility of enacting the offering analogy a source of joy for himself and the Philippians? (2:17, 18; see v. 12)

 FAITH ALIVE

"Commit yourself to obedience. Allow God's work of salvation to have its full work in you. Recognize that your whole Christian life, from being *willing* to *doing it,* is all God's work." [6]

In what areas of your Christian life do you need to guard against complaining and disputing?

In which of your activities or contacts with the world are you most likely to shine as light in the darkness?

What leaders in the past or present have served you or your church so devotedly that their lives were poured out like a drink offering on yours?

REJOICE IN SELF-SACRIFICE

Philippians is a letter in which Paul held up several examples for his readers to follow. The primary pattern was the Lord Jesus, but there were others who followed Jesus so well that they, too, could be examples.

Why was Paul wanting to send Timothy to Philippi? (Phil. 2:19)

When did he plan to send Timothy? (v. 23)

What qualities that Timothy had demonstrated in his ministry with Paul were ones that Paul had already stressed in Philippians? Try to align verses from the epistle with your answers.

Who was Epaphroditus? (v. 25; 4:18)

Why was Paul sending Epaphroditus home to Philippi? (vv. 26, 28)

How did Epaphroditus's life illustrate the qualities of humility, obedience, and self-sacrifice that Paul wanted the Philippians to have? (vv. 25–30)

How does the honor Paul asked the Philippians to bestow on Epaphroditus (v. 29) relate to the honor God bestows on Christ? (vv. 9–11)

FAITH ALIVE

Humility eventually must express itself in service of real people. Service is never convenient. Some measure of self-sacrifice is required. The greatest servants sacrifice the most of their own conveniences and pleasures.

Who personifies for you humility, service, and self-sacrifice as Timothy and Epaphroditus did for the Philippians?

What specifically have you learned from this person or these persons?

Every generation of Christian believers looks to the one before for Christ-like examples. This means that God may expect you to be an example of His Son's humility, obedience, and self-sacrifice to someone else. Accept the challenge.

1. Aleksandr I. Solzhenitsyn, *The Gulag Archipelago,* trans. by Thomas P. Whitney. Copyright © 1973 by Aleksandr I. Solzhenitsyn. English translation copyright © 1973, 1974 by Harper & Row, Publishers, Inc., 163.

2. Ibid., 168.

3. *Spirit-Filled Life Bible* (Nashville, TN: Thomas Nelson Publishers, 1991), 1803–1804, note on 2:7.

4. Ibid., 1804, "Kingdom Dynamics: Faith Exalting Jesus' Lordship."

5. Ibid., note on 2:12.

6. Ibid., 1808, "Truth-in-Action through Philippians: How to Develop Dynamic Discipleship."

Lesson 8/Joy in Jesus: Discipline
(Phil. 3:1–21)

To let go of pride and relax in the humility of powerlessness was the key to surviving the heartlessness of the Soviet prison camp society Aleksandr Solzhenitsyn found. But surviving the body-breaking, spirit-bruising assaults of the interrogators was another matter.

"So what is the answer?" Solzhenitsyn inquired. "How can you stand your ground when you are weak and sensitive to pain, when people you love are still alive, when you are unprepared?

"What do you need to make you stronger than the interrogator and the whole trap?

"From the moment you go to prison you must put your cozy past firmly behind you. At the very threshold, you must say to yourself, 'My life is over, a little early to be sure, but there's nothing to be done about it. I shall never return to freedom. I am condemned to die—now or a little later. But later on, in truth, it will be even harder, and so the sooner the better. I no longer have any property whatsoever. For me those I love have died, and for them I have died. From today on, my body is useless and alien to me. Only my spirit and my conscience remain precious and important to me.'

"Confronted by such a prisoner, the interrogation will tremble.

"Only the man who has renounced everything can win that victory.

"But how can one turn one's body to stone?"[1]

Intense self-discipline and self-denial were the keys to surviving the brutal prison camp interrogations. During his

Roman imprisonment, Paul also found that intense discipline was an integral part of following Christ. Yet it was not self-energized discipline that Paul discovered. The apostle Paul learned the secret of total reliance on Jesus Christ. It was Jesus Christ who strengthened Paul. Fortunately the discipline of Christlikeness is a joyous discipline rather than a desperate one such as Solzhenitsyn had to learn. It is a discipline produced by the power of the Holy Spirit at work in the believer's life and not a self-induced discipline manufactured by mere human will.

REJOICE IN HARDSHIP

Paul began the third chapter of Philippians with an assertion that rejoicing in the Lord was protection against the joyless false teaching of legalistic Judaizers who put a veneer of grace language over their dependence on the Law.

Why did Paul use such strong expressions in Philippians 3:2 in condemning these Judaizers?

Beware of dogs (see Gal. 5:15)

Beware of evil workers (see Gal. 1:8, 9; 4:17; 5:4)

Beware of the mutilation (see Gal. 5:12; 6:12)

How did Paul characterize the true faith of the Philippians in contrast to the false doctrine of the Judaizers? (Phil. 3:3)

BEHIND THE SCENES

Paul refused to let *circumcision* become a bad word because circumcision was from God as a sign of membership in the covenant people (Gen. 17:9–14). He insisted that physical circumcision had never been enough to mark a person as a member of the covenant people (Rom. 2:28, 29; 9:6–8). Real circumcision had always involved the heart. If there was no heart response to God with the same faith that Abraham had exercised toward God, there was no true circumcision.

Paul insisted that every believer in Jesus is "circumcised" (Phil 3:3; Col. 2:11), that is, marked as a member of the new covenant people of Christ. Philippians 3:3 associates this circumcision of the heart with the Holy Spirit, probably in the sense that the presence of the Spirit is the seal of God's redemption (Eph. 1:13). Colossians 2:11, 12 associates this circumcision of the heart with Christ and baptism as a representation of resurrection with Christ to newness of life (see Rom. 6:4).

Why did Paul consider himself a qualified spokesman about the spiritual dangers of putting "confidence in the flesh"? (Phil 3:4–6)

How could Paul conclude that all the assets of his Jewish background were liabilities as far as Christ was concerned? (vv. 7, 8)

In general terms, what had Paul come to prefer to confidence in the flesh? (vv. 8, 9)

FAITH ALIVE

Steps to Dynamic Devotion. Devotion focuses on the pursuit of intimacy with God. It is "devoting oneself" to knowing Jesus Christ. One measure of maturity is the degree to which this pursuit becomes our consuming focus and desire. Nowhere is the disciple of Jesus more challenged to become a man or woman "after God's own heart" than here.

Understand that no personal achievements earn spiritual position. Do not be afraid to lose everything in your quest to know Christ [Phil. 3:7–9]. Make "knowing" Christ your main goal in life. Know that this quest always involves sacrifice and unselfish living.[2]

Specifically, what three phases of Christian discipline were parts of Paul's supreme desire to know Christ? (Phil. 3:10)

1. (see Eph. 1:15–23)

2. (see Phil. 1:29; 2 Tim. 3:12)

3. (see Rom. 8:36; 2 Cor. 4:10)

What was the goal of Paul's disciplined desire to know Christ fully? (Phil. 3:11)

BEHIND THE SCENES

Paul's expression, "If, by any means, I may attain to the resurrection from the dead," is not intended to communicate doubt about *whether* he would participate in the resurrection.

The only question is the *manner* in which he would experience resurrection. Because of his pending trial, Paul had to take into account the possibility of imminent execution. Because he expected to be released after his trial, Paul had a hope of living until the Lord returned.[3] Until he experienced the resurrection, in whatever form, Paul disciplined himself to pursue the knowledge of Christ with all his energy.

 ### FAITH ALIVE

"Now no chastening [discipline] seems to be joyful for the present, but painful" (Heb. 12:11). The joy is never in the hardship; it is always and only in fellowshiping with Jesus.

How can difficult or adverse circumstances be turned into opportunities to trust God more completely in your life?

What things are you tempted to trust for security and a sense of accomplishment rather than Jesus?

How can you allow the Holy Spirit to help you to know the power of Christ's resurrection, the fellowship of His suffering, and conformity to His death?

REJOICE IN HARDSHIP

In spite of all of the hardship Paul had endured in his years as an apostle, eager to serve the Lord Jesus where no one else had proclaimed the gospel, he could not claim to have arrived at spiritual maturity. Paul, the model prisoner of the Lord, could only call for total faith and trust in Jesus Christ on his own part and on the part of his readers. Paul's secret was knowing firsthand the power of Jesus Christ at work in adverse circumstances.

What was it that Paul was striving for in his spiritual life? (Phil. 3:12)

WORD WEALTH

Perfected, *teleioo* (Phil. 3:12). To complete, accomplish, carry through to the end, bring to a successful conclusion, reach a goal, fulfill. In an ethical and spiritual sense, the word signifies a bringing to maturity, a perfecting.[4]

In order to meet the challenges of spiritual discipline, what were Paul's attitudes toward the past and future? (3:13)

What was Paul's spiritual goal? (3:14)

BEHIND THE SCENES

In Philippians 3:13, 14, Paul used one of his favorite metaphors, the footrace, to illustrate the endurance needed to live the Christian life. The runner must not look back but focus on the part of the race yet to be run. His ultimate focus is on the finish line and, if he is used to winning, on the prize that he can claim.

The calling a person receives from God is both a calling to salvation and a calling to spiritual maturity. Most people don't realize when they trust Christ as Savior that they have also entered a long-distance race toward Christlikeness. When they do realize it, they also recognize that the prize is more than worth the effort.

According to Philippians 3:15, 16, describe Paul's appeal for a united commitment to spiritual discipleship.

The need for maturity

God's role in unity

Ways to express unity

 FAITH ALIVE

Steps to Dynamic Devotion (Phil. 3:12–19). Devotion focuses on the pursuit of intimacy with God. Aim to achieve the goal God has set for you. Spare no cost in this quest. Spare no effort in your pressing toward the mark of knowing Christ. Recognize that a single-eyed pursuit of God is the hallmark of true spiritual maturity. Know that those who offer cheap alternatives to knowing Christ become His enemies.[5]

FAITH ALIVE

Endurance calls for inner fortitude and commitment, but it makes all the difference in the world what one is enduring for. Enduring the last few days before a root canal job is torture; enduring the last few days before Christmas is a breeze. No matter how much endurance your Christian life demands, the prize at the end of the race makes it worthwhile.

In what ways has your Christian life required the endurance of a long-distance runner?

How have you found Jesus to be the greatest encouragement to persevere in following Him in the race of life? (see Heb. 12:1, 2)

How have you found unity with your brothers and sisters in Christ to be helpful in persevering in the race of the Christian life?

REJOICE IN HEAVEN

Spiritual discipline does involve denying oneself, and it does require endurance, but its rewards are both earthly and heavenly. The transformation spiritual discipline makes in life on earth is preparation for the transformation the Lord Jesus Christ will make to prepare His followers for life with Him in eternity. In Philippians 3:17, Paul added himself to those whom the Philippians were to imitate. Who else had Paul commended as examples?

2:5–11

2:19–24

2:25–30

Why were the Philippians to avoid the example set by those whom Paul called "the enemies of the cross of Christ"? (3:18, 19)

What major contrast did Paul establish between "the enemies of the cross of Christ" and the Philippian believers? (3:19, 20)

    BEHIND THE SCENES

Philippi was a Roman colony, which means that it was settled by veterans of the Roman army as an outpost of Roman civilization in the province of Macedonia. Its residents had been granted Roman citizenship, which was a rare status for provincial residents. The goal of Roman policy was that Philippi and similar colonies scattered about the provinces would promote political and social stability throughout the farflung empire.

The residents of Philippi gained a great deal of prestige among neighboring communities, as well as legal advantages over them because of their status as Roman citizens. They understood certain things when Paul spoke of a higher citizenship in the kingdom of heaven. They understood that heavenly responsibilities went along with heavenly privileges. They understood that citizens should declare their citizenship by means of their behavior.

How should good citizens of a kingdom prepare for a long-expected visit from the king?

How should citizens of the kingdom of heaven prepare for the long-expected return of "their King," the Lord Jesus Christ? (Phil. 3:20)

When the Lord Jesus Christ returns to earth, what will He do for those who are citizens of heaven? (v. 21)

 ### FAITH ALIVE

Citizenship is usually taken for granted by those who were born citizens of a country. Naturalized citizens who obtained citizenship in a country of their choice typically value it more, and citizens who live away from their country in a struggling one grow to prize citizenship.

What cost was involved in getting your citizenship in heaven? How was it paid?

How does your citizenship in heaven and your earthly national citizenship interact? (see Matt. 22:17–21)

How does the Savior's final work for you as a citizens of heaven (3:20, 21) relate to the work of discipline you are to engage in while waiting for Him? (Rom. 12:1, 2)

1. Aleksandr I. Solzhenitsyn, *The Gulag Archipelago,* Vol. 1, trans. by Thomas P. Whitney. Copyright © 1973 by Aleksandr I. Solzenhitsyn. English translation copyright © 1973, 1974 by Harper & Row, Publishers, Inc., 124.

2. *Spirit-Filled Life Bible* (Nashville, TN: Thomas Nelson Publishers, 1991), 1809, "Truth-in-Action through Philippians: Steps to Dynamic Devotion."

3. Homer A. Kent, Jr., "Philippians," *The Expositor's Bible Commentary,* Vol. 11 (Grand Rapids, MI: Zondervan Publishing House, 1978), 142.

4. *Spirit-Filled Life Bible,* 1928, "Word Wealth: 3:12 perfected."

5. Ibid., 1809, "Truth in-Action through Philippians: Steps to Dynamic Devotion."

Lesson 9/Joy in Goodness
(Phil. 4:1–23)

A widow woman lived in a cottage in the forest. In front of her cottage stood two lovely rose bushes. One bore white roses and the other red ones. The widow had two beautiful daughters, one dark and one fair, whom she named in honor of the blossoms on the rose bushes. The fair one called Snow White was gentle and quiet, and the dark one called Rose Red was more adventurous, preferring to spend her time outdoors.

The sisters were as good as they were lovely, devoted to one another and their poor mother. One bitter winter's night a bear knocked on their door and asked to warm himself by the fire. In spite of their fear, the woman and her daughters allowed the wretched creature in. Every night the bear returned to sleep by their fire until he disappeared in the spring.

Three times during the next summer Snow White and Rose Red had encounters with an unpleasant and ungrateful dwarf. The first time they rescued him when his beard became caught in a crack in the log he was trying to split. Next time the dwarf's beard was tangled in his fishing line as a large fish pulled him toward the water. Finally Snow White and Rose Red rescued the dwarf from an eagle that was carrying him away.

In each incident the girls were genuinely concerned for the cranky little man's welfare. Each time the dwarf complained about how the sisters saved him. He carried away a bag of gold or jewels in each instance without any thanks or gifts of gratitude.

As the eagle flew away after the third rescue, a black bear burst from the brush and made for the dwarf. "Don't eat me," he cried. "Eat the two plump little girls instead." The bear struck the dwarf dead with one blow of his mighty paw.

The bear turned instantly into a handsome prince. The wicked dwarf had placed him under a spell years before and stolen his treasure. The prince married Snow White and his brother wed Rose Red. Their mother moved to the palace as well, and she brought with her the two rose bushes, one white and the other red.[1]

There is a power in goodness that exceeds the expectations of every person who believes the Devil's lie that a little selfish scheming is necessary to succeed. Goodness demands both the purity of Snow White to choose what is right and the passion of Rose Red to persevere in the face of wickedness.

PEACE IS GOOD

Two women at Philippi who may have once been as devoted to one another as Snow White and Rose Red became enemies, and the whole church vibrated from their division. Without the goodness of peace, no other goodness could flourish in the Philippian church.

What was Paul's opinion of the Philippian church? (4:1)

Why did it distress Paul to hear that there was division between two of his former coworkers at Philippi? (v. 2)

What appeal did Paul make to an anonymous "true companion" in Philippians 4:3?

If Philippians 4:4–7 is addressed particularly to Euodia, Syntyche, and Paul's "true companion," what spiritual deficiencies were contributing to their divisiveness?

How do you think continual rejoicing in the Lord contributes to peace between Christians? (v. 4)

How do you think a spirit of gentleness contributes to peace between Christians? (v. 5)

 WORD WEALTH

Gentleness, *epieikes.* Suggests a character that is equitable, reasonable, forbearing, moderate, fair, and considerate. Gentleness in a personality is the opposite of harsh, abrasive, sarcastic, cruel, and contentious.[2] A gentle person is gracious toward others, including those who hold different opinions.

How do you think anticipating the imminent return of the Lord contributes to peace between Christians? (Phil. 4:5)

How do you think anxiety about life contributes to friction between Christians? (v. 6)

WORD WEALTH

To be anxious, *merimnao.* Derived from a word that means "to divide." Anxiety is the emotional state of distraction caused by worry about too many things or the wrong things. Anxiety divides up the emotional and physical resources of a person into so many pieces that he or she cannot focus enough energy to deal effectively with the demands of life.

Anxiety is characterized by stress and pressure. Jesus warned against squandering the energy of life meant for coping with today's problems in worrying about tomorrow before it ever arrives (Matt. 6:34). The peace of God enables a Christian to focus on today with today's energy.

How do you think grateful prayer contributes to peace between Christians? (Phil. 4:6)

        BEHIND THE SCENES

"*Supplication* is more than petitioning, but suggests an intensity of earnestness in extended prayer—not to gain merit by many words, but to fully transfer the burden of one's soul into God's hands. Prayer and peace are closely connected. One who entrusts cares to Christ instead of fretting over them will experience the peace of God to guard him from nagging anxiety."[3]

How do you think peace with God contributes to peace between Christians? (Phil. 4:7)

FAITH ALIVE

Jesus pronounced a blessing on peacemakers (Matt. 5:9) and promised a quality of inner peace that the world can never give (John 14:27). Peace is truly one of the greatest blessings of the Christian life.

How have you seen a disagreement between two people disturb an entire group?

How have you seen the Lord use a peacemaker to bring reconciliation and unity between two or more estranged Christians?

How have you found that extended prayer relieves anxiety in your life and restores your peace with God?

PURITY IS GOOD

Peace and purity are spiritually related. Impurity agitates the spirit and mind and reduces peace. Purity calms the spirit and mind and leads to inner tranquillity. What do you think Paul meant when he told the Philippian believers to "meditate on these things," namely on subjects possessing the qualities listed in Philippians 4:8?

There are eight good qualities of "food for thought" listed in Philippians 4:8. The last two terms in the list are general qualities that conclude the list by meaning "and anything else like these other traits." "Any virtue" and "anything praiseworthy" (4:8) can serve as categories by which to group the other six terms listed in the verse.[4] With the aid of the accompanying Scripture portions, define the terms of Christian meditation.

"ANY VIRTUE"

"Whatever things *are* true" (Eph. 4:15, 21, 25)

"Whatever things *are* noble" (Col. 3:1, 2)

"Whatever things *are* just" (Rom. 12:3; James 2:1, 12, 13)

"Whatever things *are* pure" (James 1:27; 1 John 3:3)

"ANYTHING PRAISEWORTHY"

"Whatever things *are* lovely" (1 Cor. 13:4–7; 1 Tim. 1:5)

"Whatever things *are* of good report" (Heb. 11:1, 2; James 3:17, 18)

FAITH ALIVE

How to Develop Dynamic Discipleship (Phil. 2:2; 4:8, 9). Discipleship is apprenticeship to the life of Jesus, focusing on Christ as Mentor and Model. . . . Discipleship may call the Christian to choose to lay aside rights much valued in our culture, and to accept the life-role assigned by God. This role may not appear to be a place of acknowledgement, but trust God to choose how to establish and promote you.

Seek to maintain unity with other believers in your thoughts, attitudes, love, spirit, and purpose [2:2]. . . . Determine your own thought life [4:8, 9]. Do not let others do it for you. Cause your mind to dwell on those things that bring peace to you and glory to God. Follow holy leadership as a pattern for life and faith.[5]

Philippians 4:6, 7 showed what to do to experience the protection of the peace of God. According to verse 9, what should the Philippian believers do to experience the presence of "the God of peace"?

What is the connection between the things to be meditated on in Philippians 4:8 and the things Paul had modeled for the Philippians in verse 9?

   FAITH ALIVE

The presence of the peace of God depends on the unity of believers and freedom from the anxiety attendant upon divisiveness, but the presence of the God of peace depends on the purity of one's thoughts. Peace and purity are two great goods of Christian experience that cannot be separated. What are the influences in your life that tend to introduce impure subjects into your thinking?

How do these impure thoughts interfere with your fellowship with the God of peace?

How can you reduce the influence of the sources of impure thoughts and increase your exposure to virtuous and praiseworthy sources of thoughts?

From your personal experience, can you name a person who modeled a way of thinking that made it seem like the God of peace was with that person?

GENEROSITY IS GOOD

A person at peace with God and others is a person whose interpersonal relationships are open for giving and receiving acts of love. A person whose mind is focused on what is virtuous and praiseworthy wants to enjoy giving and receiving love. Both peace and purity lead to generosity.

Paul rejoiced in the generosity of the Philippian church. What had been their record of generosity to Paul? (Phil. 4:10, 15, 16, 18; see 2:25)

What spiritual benefits had Paul gained from being completely dependent on the generosity of other Christians? (Phil. 4:11–13)

FAITH ALIVE

Riches Are Not to Be Trusted (Phil. 4:12, 13). Let this scripture be a guiding light to understanding God's will on the subject of prosperity. It tells us yes (we can have riches), and no (do not trust in them). With the mind of Christ (see Phil. 2:1–5), we will never become high-minded if blessed with wealth. Here is assurance that if our lives are geared to the Word of God, then, through Christ, we can experience either financial wealth or temporary setback, but we will still be steadfast in our living, all because our trust will be only in Him.[6]

What spiritual benefits for the Philippians did Paul foresee growing out of their pattern of generosity toward him? (4:14, 17, 19)

Why do you think God alone is to be praised for generosity given and received and for lessons learned from giving and receiving? (4:20)

FAITH ALIVE

Do Whatever He Says; Then You Will Prosper (Phil. 4:19). This verse tells us that God will supply our need by a distinct and definite measure, "according to His riches." In declaring this, God makes clear that He is not stingy when it comes to provision. His "riches" encompass all of creation, so there is nothing you need that He cannot provide!

Do not misquote or misread this verse. It does not say that God shall supply your <u>needs</u>; it says that He shall supply [provide for] your <u>need</u>. That includes everything at once, and all of it is adequately covered because He does it according to His riches.

This verse cannot be lifted out of the Bible. It underwrites and relates to everything the Scriptures tell us to do in order to prosper. If we do what the Bible tells us to do, then God will provide abundantly.[7]

What reasons for joy on Paul's part are contained in the greeting and blessing of Philippians? (4:21–23)

FAITH ALIVE

Paul rejoiced to contemplate the Philippian believers experiencing peace, purity, and generosity. You can rejoice as well while the Holy Spirit uses the Word of God to create these qualities in your life.

What spiritual lessons can you learn only during times of financial needs?

What spiritual lessons can you learn only during times of financial plenty?

What spiritual lessons can you learn only by giving generously to others in need?

What spiritual lessons can you learn only by receiving the generosity of others when you are in need?

1. "Snow White and Rose Red," *The Complete Fairy Tales of the Brothers Grimm,* trans. by Jack Zipes (Toronto: Bantam Books, 1987), 516–521.
2. *Spirit-Filled Life Bible* (Nashville, TN: Thomas Nelson Publishers, 1991), 1843, "Word Wealth: 3:3 gentleness."
3. Ibid., 1806, note on 4:6, 7.
4. J. B. Lightfoot, *St. Paul's Epistle to the Philippians* (Grand Rapids, MI: Zondervan Publishing House, 1953), 161.
5. *Spirit-Filled Life Bible,* 1808, "Truth-in-Action through Philippians: How to Develop Dynamic Discipleship."
6. Ibid., 1807, "Kingdom Dynamics: Riches Are Not to Be Trusted."
7. Ibid., "Kingdom Dynamics: Do Whatever He Says; Then You Will Prosper."

Lesson 10/Jesus: Supreme in Everything
(Col. 1:1–29)

During the Dark Ages of western Europe a brilliant civilization sparkled in the Byzantine Empire, the eastern remnant of the empire that had been Rome. "Byzantine" remains in the English language as an adjective that suggests something incomprehensibly complicated, mysterious, and perhaps sinister. In Byzantium, the politics, social customs, morals, and religions of east and west met and merged in sometimes fantastic forms.

Before the Gothic style emerged with its vertical lines reaching for the heavens, Byzantine architecture produced the most magnificent churches of the Mediterranean world. The floor plan was based on the shape of the cross. Columns supported vaulted ceilings, and a large central dome spanned the open space created by the intersection of the arms of the cross.

The chief decorative art form of Byzantine churches consisted of mosaic depictions of biblical characters and events. From every available space around the roofline and in the ceiling vaults and domes, color blazed with an oriental love of bright hues to make a visual Bible for the illiterate masses. Certain major biblical themes appeared in the same place in most churches.

The central dome in a Byzantine church held the largest and most important mosaic. They called it *Christos Pantokrater*, "Christ, the All-Powerful." This depiction of Christ communicated majesty and holiness. All around the church scenes of His gentleness and mercy glowed in the candlelight, but looming above all and peering down through clouds of incense on every worshiper was the awesome, sovereign Lord.

LIVE TO PLEASE JESUS

The awesome, sovereign Lord of the universe has chosen to call people to Himself rather than to force them to submit to Him. He wants voluntary subjects who will live for Him because they love Him and appreciate the salvation from sins He died to provide for them.

 ### BEHIND THE SCENES

About one hundred miles inland from Ephesus in western Asia Minor, three towns clustered in the Lycus River valley. Laodicea was a major city; Hierapolis was a good-sized and growing town; but Colosse was small, the smallest town to which Paul wrote an epistle. Once it had been large and important, but in the first century A.D. the prosperity of Laodicea and Hierapolis was rapidly dooming Colosse.

The churches of Hierapolis and Laodicea (Col. 2:1; 4:13, 16; Rev. 3:14–22) endured long after Colosse ceased to exist, but in the first century Colosse was the spiritual leader of the three. That two epistles destined to Colosse (Colossians and Philemon) appear in the pages of the New Testament speaks highly of the spiritual prominence of little Colosse.

From Colossians 1:1, 2, analyze the salutation of the epistle.

The senders

The recipients

The opening salute (see 4:18)

From Colossians 1:3–5, describe Paul's thanksgiving to God for the Colossian Christians (see 1 Cor. 13:13).

About their faith

About their love

About their hope

Describe the experience of the Colossians with the gospel of Christ. (1:5–7)

What was Epaphras's role in the church of Colosse? (1:7, 8; 4:12, 13)

Describe Paul's prayer for the Colossians in Colossians 1:9–12.

For knowledge

For behavior

For strength

For thanksgiving

How had the Colossians been moved from the kingdom of darkness to the kingdom of light? (1:12–14)

FAITH ALIVE

People of the Kingdom (Col. 1:13). The "transference" of the believer, from under Satan's authority to Christ's, is described as movement into another "kingdom." Ensuing verses describe Christ's redemption as bringing us to a place of "completeness," that is, of spiritual adequacy, authority, or ability to live victoriously over and above the invisible powers of darkness (vv. 14–16; 2:6–10).

This becomes functionally true, as opposed to merely theoretically so, when we 1) live and love as <u>citizens</u> of the heavenly kingdom (Phil. 3:20); 2) utilize this kingdom's <u>currency</u>, which is of irresistible value (Acts 3:6); 3) operate as <u>ambassadors</u> authorized to offer kingdom peace and reconciliation to those yet unrenewed in Christ (2 Cor. 5:20); and 4) serve as the kingdom *militia*, girded for prayerful conflict against the dark powers controlling so much of this present world (Eph. 6:10–20). The terminology of "the kingdom" holds more than poetic pictures. It is practically applicable to all our living.[1]

WORD WEALTH

Blood, *haima* (Col. 1:14). The ordinary word for the complex red fluid that moves through the veins of people and animals. In the Bible *blood* is used in two special ways. First, the murder of one person by another is the shedding of blood which cries out (Gen. 4:10) for vengeance (9:6) from the ground which it defiles (Num. 35:33). Second, atonement for sin can only be made by the shedding of blood (Heb. 9:7, 11–15, 22).

The point of both special uses of the term *blood* is that "the life of all flesh is its blood" (Lev. 17:14). *Blood* is a powerful verbal symbol for life. "The soul who sins shall die" (Ezek. 18:4) unless a sacrifice gives its life by shedding its blood in his place. Under the old covenant, the blood of animals covered sins in anticipation of the sacrifice that would remove sins.

The blood of Christ represented the life of the infinite sinless Lamb of God. His blood could pay the price for an infinite number of souls who had earned death by their sins. Jesus laid down His life by spilling His blood that spiritually dead sinners might live forever.

FAITH ALIVE

The supremacy of Jesus begins in our experience as the supremacy of the salvation He shed His blood to provide and the wonderful life He enables His followers to live day by day.

What new spiritual insight has the Lord given you recently that has had an impact on how you live?

What fruitful good work has the Lord led you to engage in recently?

How have you recently experienced strengthening with the power of God for patience and longsuffering?

EVERYTHING BELONGS TO JESUS

At the edge of time, before the Son veiled His glory in order to interact with humans and show us what the Father is like, He was the Creator. He was "the brightness of [God's] glory and the express image of His person, and upholding all things by the word of His power" (Heb. 1:3). When Paul called Christ "the image of the invisible God" (Col. 1:15), what do you think he meant?

In terms of being "the image of the invisible God"

In terms of being "the express image of His person"

When Paul called Christ "the firstborn over all creation" (Col. 1:15), what do you think he meant?

In terms of genealogy

In terms of position

WORD WEALTH

Firstborn, *prototokos.* "Firstborn over all creation" does not mean that Christ was the earliest created being. *Firstborn* relates Christ to God as His Son rather than as a creature. The term *firstborn* connects Paul's thought with John's description of Jesus as "the Word" who was God (John 1:1) and was "the only begotten of the Father" (v. 14). *Firstborn* also took the first-century Jewish readers back to the language of the Greek Old Testament (Ps. 89:26, 27).

What did Christ create? (Col. 1:16)

How is Christ's role in creation clarified by each of these expressions in Colossians 1:16, 17?

"All things were created . . . through Him"

"All things were created . . . for Him"

"He is before all things"

"In Him all things consist" (see Heb. 1:3)

BEHIND THE SCENES

Organized Structure in the Angelic Realm (Col. 1:16). There is an organized structure in the angelic realm. Profoundly influential in humanity's history, angels are involved according to their designated ranks. Though opinion differs as to the placement of angelic offices, it is clear that the angelic host are part of a highly organized world of [angelic] beings.

For example, Daniel 10:13 shows that warring angels have a chief prince, Michael, who is also called an archangel, that is, one who rules over others. Seraphim and cherubim seem to be of a slightly lower rank, just ahead of the ministering spirits (Heb. 1:14). However, it may be that the seraphim and cherubim fill a leadership role in worship while Michael leads the warring angels.

As to the dark angels, Ephesians 6:12 offers insight into the ranks of the evil angelic realm: principalities, powers, rulers of the darkness of this world, and spiritual wickedness in high places. From the information the Bible gives, we can see that the angelic realm is a distinctly structured society with different levels of authority or power endowed to each according to God's creative order.[2]

Of what else other than the physical and spiritual realms is Christ the creator? (Col. 1:18)

How did Christ initiate this new creation? (Col. 1:18)

What does Christ deserve for His creative roles in the first and second creations? (Col. 1:18)

AT A GLANCE

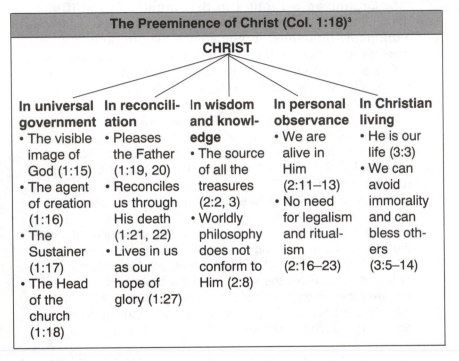

The Preeminence of Christ (Col. 1:18)[3]				
CHRIST				
In universal government	**In reconciliation**	**In wisdom and knowledge**	**In personal observance**	**In Christian living**
• The visible image of God (1:15)	• Pleases the Father (1:19, 20)	• The source of all the treasures (2:2, 3)	• We are alive in Him (2:11–13)	• He is our life (3:3)
• The agent of creation (1:16)	• Reconciles us through His death (1:21, 22)	• Worldly philosophy does not conform to Him (2:8)	• No need for legalism and ritualism (2:16–23)	• We can avoid immorality and can bless others (3:5–14)
• The Sustainer (1:17)	• Lives in us as our hope of glory (1:27)			
• The Head of the church (1:18)				

From Colossians 1:19, 20, describe what pleased the Father about the Son.

Regarding His nature

Regarding His ministry

Regarding His sacrifice

WORD WEALTH

Eight of the seventeen New Testament occurrences of the term *fullness* are in Colossians. In Colossians 1:19 *fullness* refutes an idea of the false teachers operating in Colosse. They used *fullness* to encompass a hierarchy of spirit beings and gods. In their doctrine, humankind was on the bottom rung of a spiritual pecking order, and God was on the top. In between was this *fullness* of intermediaries that people had to deal with.

Paul dismissed the spiritual rigmarole of the false teachers by claiming that "all the fullness should dwell" in Christ. All of the spiritual qualities and attributes that bridge the gap between finite people and the infinite God are in Christ. Nothing else and no one else is needed.[4]

From Colossians 1:21–23, describe the complete process of the salvation of the Colossians.

Their former condition

Their regeneration

Their future goal

Their present perseverance

BEHIND THE SCENES

The Greek language of the New Testament had several ways of expressing the "if . . ., then . . ." conditional thought. Conditional expressions in the New Testament range from those whose conditions are certain to be met to those whose conditions are certain not to be met. "If indeed you continue in the faith" (Col. 1:23) sets out the condition of faithfulness in a grammatical form that assumes that Christians will meet it.

FAITH ALIVE

Everything belongs to the Lord Jesus Christ. First He carried out the plans of the Father in creating the physical and spiritual worlds. Later He carried out the Father's plans in redeeming men and women to establish a new creation, the church, of which He is Head.

What do you find to be the most awe-inspiring concept in Colossians 1:15–23? Why?

In contemplating the preeminent Christ, what encouragement do you find for persevering in your faith and in the hope of the gospel?

DIRECT EVERYONE TO JESUS

Jesus is supreme in everything. We are to live to please Him in all things. All the fullness of God resides in Him who is the creator of all things and the re-creator of people ruined by sin who come to Him in faith. It follows that believers in Jesus have a responsibility to point other people ruined by sin to the One who can reconcile them to God.

How had Paul come to understand his sufferings as part of his ministry for Christ? (Col. 1:24; see Phil. 1:29)

In Colossians 1:25–27, how did Paul describe the ministry God gave him among the Gentiles?

The stewardship from God

The nature of a mystery

The reason for revealing the mystery

The content of this mystery

From Colossians 1:28, describe the preaching of Paul.

Its aspects

Its goal

By what standard did Paul measure the effort he put into proclaiming the gospel of Christ? (Col. 1:29; see v. 11 and Eph. 1:19, 20)

 FAITH ALIVE

Terminology of the Kingdom in Paul's Writings (Col. 1:27, 28). "In Christ" is the expression Paul most frequently uses to designate the new life potential through the gospel. The Messiah (Christ) being King, the term clearly places the believer in the circle of all that is represented and contained in the King, His salvation conquest, and His personal rule.

The essential truth is that the Savior-King has come, and in Him the rule of God has altered the limits sin has heretofore placed on individuals. People no longer need to be ruled by their carnality (flesh) or controlled by evil (the Devil). Being freed, that is, transferred to a new kingdom, they can know the joy of a relationship with God through the power of the Cross and can realize a beginning reinstatement of their rulership under God, through the power of the Holy Spirit.

Thereby, living in the King's kingdom brings a dual hope: eternity with Christ and the promise of grace to begin "reigning in life." Now, "in Christ" designates the new life that may be lived in the benefits of, and by the power of, the King Jesus, "who has brought life [reigning in life presently in Christ—Rom. 5:8] and immortality [reigning forever with Christ—Rev. 22:5] to light through the gospel" (2 Tim. 1:10).[5]

 ## FAITH ALIVE

Paul presented his commitment to presenting "every man perfect in Christ Jesus" (Col. 1:28) to the Colossian believers as an example of the urgency and power that should characterize their witness for Christ. Because Jesus is Lord and supreme in everything, you too should want to direct your unbelieving friends and acquaintances to Him.

What aspects of the gospel do you think are "mysteries" to the unbelievers whom you know?

When you are afraid or reluctant to give your personal testimony of faith in Christ or to share the gospel, what can you remind yourself of concerning God's desire for your friends to know Christ (Col. 1:27) and about the power available to you for witnessing? (v. 29)

1. *Spirit-Filled Life Bible* (Nashville, TN: Thomas Nelson Publishers, 1991), 1813, "Kingdom Dynamics: People of the Kingdom."

2. Ibid., 1814, "Kingdom Dynamics: Organized Structure in the Angelic Realm."

3. Ibid., Chart: "The Preeminence of Christ."

4. Ibid., note on 1:19.

5. Ibid., 1815, "Kingdom Dynamics: Paul's Writings."

Lesson 11/Jesus: Supreme in Spirituality
(Col. 2:1–23)

Hans worried and worried. How should he act when he saw the king? He had danced for joy when the village schoolmaster chose him to represent the children of the village in the celebration of the five hundredth anniversary of the kingdom, but now he just worried.

Hans asked the old men in the village square, "How should I act when I see the king?" One said that Hans should bow to the ground every ten feet as he approached the throne. Another said he should keep his eyes on the ground and kiss the king's hand when he held it out. Still a third said he needed to learn the official way to address the king, which the old man couldn't remember any longer but maybe the parish priest knew.

The priest in his robe looked startled when Hans rocketed around the corner of the rectory and bumped into him. "Please, Father Gruber, tell me how to address the king when I represent the children at the festival," Hans panted.

Father Gruber copied down a long salutation in a form of the language no one used any more except some people way up in the mountains. Hans took it home and practiced it until he knew it by heart, although he didn't understand parts of it.

When the big day came, Hans stood in a procession of dignitaries waiting for their audiences with the king. He felt very insignificant among the noblemen, knights, and lovely ladies, so he closed his eyes and imagined over and over how he would walk and bow, kneel and kiss, and solemnly address the king.

After a long wait, but also all at once, the massive doors opened without a sound to reveal the king seated in state at the far end of the most beautiful room Hans had ever seen. A hundred pairs of eyes watched him forget everything he had practiced a thousand times. Hans had never seen the king before, only his portraits. He could not take his eyes off that grave and noble face whose eyes looked right through him.

With a lurch and a stagger Hans started forward. His mouth hung open and the spray of flowers dragged on the floor at his side. He couldn't take his eyes off the eyes of the king all the way to the foot of the throne, and then he couldn't remember anything to say.

Hans reached out the flowers to the king and opened his mouth. His voice squeaked, "The children all love you, your Majesty," and he hung his head in shame to cry as the dignitaries clapped and the king smiled.

BATTLE OF THE AGES

Do we worship God acceptably by keeping rules and observing rituals or do we worship Him acceptably with love and devotion from a pure heart? There are always those who want to set up their way as the way to approach God and substitute their traditions for the simple gospel of the New Testament. It was true then and there in Colosse; it is true here and now.

From Colossians 2:1–3, describe the outcome Paul desired from the conflict he had for the Christians in Colosse and Laodicea.

In unity

In spiritual understanding

How were the opponents of the true gospel attempting to lure away the Colossians? (vv. 4, 8)

What did Paul recommend to the Colossian Christians as the way to resist falsehood and remain in the truth? (vv. 6, 7, 9, 10)

Who did Paul say was ultimately behind the attempts to pervert the gospel of Christ? (vv. 10, 15)

 ### BEHIND THE SCENES

What about Mind Control and Mind-Science Beliefs? (Col. 2:8). Such cults focus on the "universal consciousness" concept that human beings 1) are part of a vast, timeless consciousness; 2) are ultimately divine; 3) will live forever in various forms (reincarnation, and so on); 4) can communicate with the dead or other spirits; and 5) can receive power through psychic or even bodily exercises to transcend nature, understand mysteries, and affect their own destinies or the lives of those around them.

These groups, in the name of "research and enlightenment," "psychic research," "transcendental meditation," "yoga," and so on, are actually not in touch with some great "God consciousness" or psychic power, but with Satan and demons.

The Greek word *psuche* is translated "soul," from which we derive the word *psychic*. Most mind-science groups deal with psychic, or soulish, phenomena. First Corinthians 2:14 says the *psuchikos* or "soulish" person ("the natural man") will not receive the things of the Spirit of God, for they are foolishness to him. Mind control and New Age movement teachings all appeal to the soulish man, because they do not require repentance and being born again (John 3:3, 5). A concept prevalent in these groups is that if a person gains sufficient knowledge, he can dominate or control events because he is *part* of god or *is* god.

We must remember that the soulish realm is the realm of demons. Demons can and often do enter into this psychic area. The people who are in touch with the dead or "the other world" are not tapping into some universal consciousness.

They are in touch with demons. Demons lurk behind many of the oriental religions, as well as behind the mind control teachings.[1]

 ## FAITH ALIVE

Little Hans looked to all the traditions and wisdom about approaching the king, but he was better off responding directly to the king. Focus on how the King has revealed Himself to you rather than on man-made or devilish schemes to replace or "supplement" the Word of God.

In what sense are "all the treasures of wisdom and knowledge" hidden in Christ? (Col. 2:3)

What human philosophies, cults, or non-Christian religions have you found attractive in the past? What was it about them that appealed to you?

How have you found "the fullness of the Godhead" and spiritual satisfaction in Christ rather than in the philosophies, cults, or non-Christian religions?

VICTORY IN THE BATTLE

The conflict between the truth that is in Jesus and the philosophies and traditions of humankind is a spiritual one that must have a spiritual resolution. All intellectual discussions about the truth of Christianity are preliminary decisions that need to lead to spiritual decisions. What human spiritual conditions did Paul represent by the terms "circumcision" and "uncircumcision"? (Col. 2:11–13)

Uncircumcision

Circumcision

How does baptism relate to the spiritual condition Paul described as "circumcision"? (vv. 11, 12)

According to Colossians 2:13–15, how did the crucifixion and resurrection of Christ cause Him to emerge victorious in the spiritual conflict?

Over sin

Over the demands of the Law

Over false teachings

 WORD WEALTH

Handwriting, *cheirographos* (Col. 2:14). "A word commonly used when a monetary obligation was acknowledged by a debtor. It means a signed confession of indebtedness, bond, or self-confessed indictment. In Ephesians 2:15 it is used of the Mosaic Law."[2]

How is the crucifixion and resurrection of Jesus a public triumph over the powers of darkness? (2:15)

FAITH ALIVE

Grounds of Authority (Col. 2:13–15). Jesus Christ's triumph over sin and evil powers was accomplished in "it"— that is, in <u>the Cross</u>. This text, joined to and studied beside others (Eph. 2:13–16; Gal. 3:13, 14; 2 Cor. 5:14–17; Rom. 5:6–15; and Rev. 12:10, 11), firmly established Jesus' suffering, shed blood, sacrificial death, and resurrection triumph as the only adequate and available grounds for ransom from sin, reconciliation to God, redemption from slavery, and restoration. The Cross is the sole hope and means for full reinstatement to relationship with God and rulership under Him—to "reign in life" (Rom. 5:17).

To avoid presumption or imbalance regarding the message and ministry of the present power of the kingdom of God, we must focus on and regularly review two points: the source and the grounds for the delegation of such authority and power. 1) God's sovereign authority and almighty power is the source from which mankind derives any ability to share in the exercise of God's kingdom power. 2) But even more important, seeing sinful, fallen man had lost all claim to his early privilege of rulership under God, let us remember the <u>grounds</u> upon which all kingdom privilege or power may be restored and by which such spiritual ministry with authority may be exercised.[3]

 FAITH ALIVE

Behind the scenes in all the spiritual conflicts you have ever known, the Lord Jesus has engaged the spiritual powers of darkness to defeat them. He has energized your spirit by means of His Spirit to emerge victorious.

Where in your life can you see evidences of life given by Christ where once there were signs of sin and death?

Write a prayer of gratitude to the Lord Jesus for removing the notice of your guilt by paying your sin debt on the Cross.

Tell about an occasion when you witnessed the forces of darkness being publicly humiliated by the truth of Christ.

LIVE LIKE VICTORS

Once it becomes clear that spiritual truth is found in Jesus rather than in human philosophy and tradition, then it should be obvious that spiritual living is also built around Him rather than around man-made codes of conduct. In fact man-made codes of conduct should be viewed skeptically as likely hindrances to Christlikeness.

What sorts of Old Testament rituals had foreshadowed the spiritual realities found in Christ? (Col. 2:16, 17)

What do you think these rituals had foretold about Christ? (vv. 16, 17)

What dangers would the Colossian Christians expose themselves to if they let others evaluate their spiritual lives by the standards of the old covenant? (v. 18)

What applications did Paul make to the Colossians' situation from the analogy of Christ as Head to the body of the church? (v. 19)

The Christian victory over sin comes from the death of Christ as the sacrifice for sin and the participation of Christians in that death (v. 12; see Rom. 6:4–11). What implications does dying with Christ have for the life of victory over sin? (vv. 20–23)

How effective are man-made rules in controlling the desires of the flesh, and why do you think this is so? (v. 23)

What do rules set up to curb the desires of the flesh actually accomplish? (v. 23)

 FAITH ALIVE

Keys to Wise Living (Col. 2:18–23). Many believers are slowed in their spiritual growth for lack of wisdom. Sometimes teaching that stymies spiritual growth is enthusiastically endorsed because believers do not know the Scriptures. We should heed Paul's warning against listening to people who pander to the flesh, rather than edifying in the truth.

Be aware that human philosophy and erroneous religious tradition are contrary to Christ. Do not be deceived. Hold fast to Christ and honor Him to please the Father. Be wise in evaluating "spiritual experiences," knowing that they are not to produce pride or elitism. Know the importance of commitment to a local church and of submission to righteous spiritual authority.[4]

FAITH ALIVE

Victorious Christian living is the responsible use of liberty governed by love for Christ and other people (Gal. 5:1, 13). It is the Holy Spirit who produces the fruit of Christlike character and behavior (vv. 16, 22–25). Rules and regulations don't result in Christlikeness.

What is the spiritual difference between abstaining from a practice as the application of a biblical principle and abstaining from a practice because someone says you have to?

How do you think the principles of death and resurrection with Christ can control the desires of the flesh if rules and regulations cannot?

If you are struggling unsuccessfully against a habitual sin of the flesh, seek the spiritual aid of your pastor or another mature Christian leader. It is not the will of the Father for you to be defeated by the flesh. Let your counselor help you find the enablement of the Holy Spirit in your conflict. The Lord may let us struggle for some time, but the struggle is part of the victory, not part of a defeat.

1. *Spirit-Filled Life Bible* (Nashville, TN: Thomas Nelson Publishers, 1991), 2006–2007, "Spiritual Answers to Hard Questions: What About Mind Control and Mind-Science Beliefs?"

2. Ibid., 1816, note on 2:14.

3. Ibid., 1816–1817, "Kingdom Dynamics: Grounds of Authority."

4. Ibid., 1820, "Truth-in-Action through Colossians: Keys to Wise Living."

Lesson 12/Jesus: Supreme in Conduct
(Col. 3:1—4:6)

When the band director came down to the junior high and asked three eighth graders to play in the Suburban High School marching band, Tim felt pretty proud of his trumpet playing. Then he and his friends found out that not enough Suburban High kids would be in the band because the football team was so bad. Who wanted to march halftime shows every week in a losing cause?

Through eight morale-sapping weeks, the story was the same except that the weather in Ohio was miserable by late October. Then, bizarrely, this same awful football team won the last two games of the season—the two most difficult games on the schedule. Of course, no one at the high school noticed, because Suburban High School students were losers and a couple of freak wins couldn't change that.

A year later when Tim was a freshman the same eleven Suburban High players who had somehow won two football games the year before won all ten of them. The next year seemed destined to turn out the same way. Now everyone came to football games, and the whole atmosphere of the high school changed. Kids wanted to be known as Suburban High students and personal friends of players on the team, which was ranked among the top ten in the state.

In fact, Country High dropped Tim's school from their schedule, and a big city school eagerly snapped up the chance to teach the country boys a lesson about real football. Every now and then Tim remembered those eight humiliating games. The night they played Big City High, it occurred to him that half of the kids in the stands—the ninth and tenth graders—had never seen Suburban High lose a game. Most of the older kids hadn't either because they had never come during the losing years.

But they didn't lose. They beat arrogant Big City High in a Pyrrhic victory that sidelined several key players with injuries. The Suburban High student body was as excited as if their team had beaten Ohio State.

The crippled team lost the next two games—the last two of the season—to the same teams that had started Suburban's glory streak two years before. Once again, no one noticed much. Suburban High School students were winners, and a couple of losses couldn't change that.

OUT WITH THE OLD

Before the Suburban High School students could take on the attitude of winners, they had to get rid of the loser's attitude they had sported for years. Before they wanted to get rid of the loser's attitude, they had to identify with a proven winner. When Christians identify wholeheartedly with their Lord, their whole attitudinal and behavioral patterns change.

Describe the union of a Christian with Christ, as outlined in Colossians 3:1–14.

In terms of mind-set

In terms of the present

In terms of the future

Paul had earlier in Colossians identified a "body of the sins of the flesh" (2:11) that needed to be put off and buried. What behavioral "members" of this body need to be put to death? (3:5)

What characteristics or motivations do these members have in common? (v. 5)

What is the danger of the activities of the members of the body of the sins of the flesh? (vv. 6, 7)

What kinds of sinful speech and sinful motives for speech did Paul command the Colossian Christians to put off? (vv. 8, 9)

What makes the "new man" in Christ truly new and different? (vv. 10, 11)

 FAITH ALIVE

Keys to Godly Relationships (Col. 3:5–11). Human relationships were designed to be fueled and filled by righteousness. To the degree we give in to the urging of our flesh nature, we will fail to experience righteous or fulfilling relationships. To the degree we practice those things God commands, our relationships will become a sampling of heaven on Earth.

Reject, turn from, and refuse to practice any form of relational unrighteousness or sin: wrong sexual activity, angry exchanges, jealous or envious attitudes, greedy desire for things, gossip, or coarse humor.[1]

 FAITH ALIVE

When we are delivered from bondage to sin and declared to be a part of the family of God, we should find a change in our hearts. No longer are we associated with the losing side of humanity. We are with Christ, the Victor.

When you think about your life right now being "hidden with Christ in God" (Col. 3:3), what are your reactions?

In terms of how you can pray

In terms of how to handle discouragement and suffering

In terms of how to trust the Holy Spirit for power for living

Since you need to put to death or put off the traits of the old man before the new man can "be renewed in knowledge according to the image of Him who created him" (Col. 3:10), how does the operation of the old man's traits interfere with the formation of the new man?

IN WITH THE NEW

Colossians 3:1—4:6 is very similar to chapters four and five of Ephesians in its emphasis on taking off the old and putting on the new, on forgiving as Christ forgave, and on family and slave-master relationships. Evidently these subjects were in the forefront of Paul's spiritual thoughts at the time he wrote these two epistles.

How did Paul characterize the Colossian Christians in their relationship to God? (Col. 3:12)

 WORD WEALTH

Chosen translates the Greek adjective *eklektos* from which English derives the word "eclectic." *Eklektos* was formed from *ek,* "out of," and *lego,* "to pick, gather." *Chosen* designates one picked out from the larger group for special service or privilege. It describes Christ as the chosen Messiah of God (Luke 23:35), angels as messengers from heaven (1 Tim. 5:21), and believers as recipients of God's favor (Matt. 24:22; Rom. 8:33; Col. 3:12). The New Testament traces the source of election to God's grace.[2]

According to Colossians 3:12, what qualities were the Colossian believers to put on like new clothes in place of the "the old man with his deeds"? (v. 9)

How to treat others

1.

2.

How to think of yourself

3.

How to react to others

4.

5.

According to Colossians 3:13, how are Christians to respond to the offenses of others?

To annoyances and inconveniences

To disloyalty and betrayal

What is the standard by which Christians are to measure their acts of forgiveness? (v. 13)

What is the belt or sash that holds all the clothes of the new man in place? (v. 14)

From Colossians 3:15, 16, describe the behavior of the new man in Christ.

In disposition

In edification

In worship

From Colossians 3:17, describe the motto of the new man in Christ.

In speech

In behavior

In attitude

 FAITH ALIVE

Steps to Dynamic Devotion (Col. 3:16, 17). Always in the New Testament, the call to wholehearted discipleship is accompanied by the call to a life of devotion. To devote is "to concentrate on a particular pursuit or purpose." A life of devotion to Christ pursues His purpose—His being reproduced in us.

Be diligent in Bible study and practice Scripture memorization and meditation. Let the Word in you produce praise to God and edification of others. Serve Jesus' purposes in every thought, word, and deed.[3]

 ## FAITH ALIVE

As people chosen by God to be His holy and beloved ones, we have ample motivation for putting on the new man in Christ. Like Tim and his classmates in the opening story, we will act out of our self-concepts. The more we associate with Jesus as Lord, the more we will desire to be like Him. Many Christians confuse forbearance and forgiveness. They think they are forgiving someone when they put up with annoying behavior. Then they refuse to forgive an intentional offense, which is when forgiveness really begins.

What are your greatest struggles with forgiveness?

Which qualities in Colossians 3:12, 14, would make you a more forgiving person?

Would you prefer the "word of Christ" to express itself more through you in the area of edification or in the area of worship? Why?

BE LIKE JESUS AT HOME

One of the primary places that our enthusiastic identification with Jesus as Lord should change our behavior is in our homes. Because it is easy to be pious in public but carnal at home, Christ hasn't really changed our lives until He is Lord of family relationships.

In Colossians 3:18, 19, what instruction did Paul give marriage partners?

Wives

Husbands

What instructions did Paul gives parents and children in Colossians 3:20, 21?

Children

Fathers

Why do you think that wives and children, those who are directed to accede to authority, are appealed to in terms of obedience to the Lord? (vv. 18, 20)

Why do you think that husbands and fathers, those who are directed to exercise authority, are warned against having or encouraging negative emotions? (vv. 19, 21)

 ### FAITH ALIVE

Husbands and Wives Called to Operate in God's Order (Col. 3:18, 19). A Christian renders service to others as a way of serving the Lord Christ. In these verses the relationship to which this truth is specifically applied is the husband-wife relationship. The role and admonition that God assigns to a husband is meant to be a way of serving his wife. Likewise a distinctive role and direction is given to the wife, according to which she serves her husband.

These roles are not self-chosen, nor are they assigned by the culture in which one lives: they are given by God as a means of manifesting the life of Christ on Earth. In this setting the word <u>submission</u> acquires its full biblical significance for family life: husband and wife alike are submissive to God in fulfilling the roles that He has given them. In serving one another, husband and wife serve and honor Christ.

The word "submit" (Greek *hupotasso*) is formed from *hupo* ("under") and *tasso* ("to arrange in an orderly manner"). In this context it describes a person who accepts his or her place under God's arranged order. Also, remember that God's directive to submit is not limited to wives. In James 4:7 and Ephesians 5:21 we see the directive applied to every believer—in his or her relationships with others—and with God.[4]

According to Colossians 3:22–25, how will the Lord repay those who serve others?

Those who serve wholeheartedly

Those who serve badly

What was to be the motive of masters for treating servants well? (4:1)

FAITH ALIVE

Your relationships with parents, marriage partner, and children are crucial forms of witness to your submission to Jesus as Lord. Likewise, your work ethics speak volumes. Whether you are a laborer, a foreman, a professional, or a corporate executive, how you treat people and how seriously you take your responsibilities set the boundaries for your Christian witness.

What can your family conclude about your relationship to the Lord Jesus from the way you treat them?

Positively

Negatively

What can your coworkers conclude about your relationship to the Lord Jesus from the way you treat people and your work responsibilities?

Positively

Negatively

What do you think the Lord would have you change?

About your family relationships

About your work relationships

BE LIKE JESUS EVERYWHERE

Once commitment to Jesus transforms the closest relationships of life, then He will revolutionize all other contacts with people. All personal contacts become opportunities and avenues for Christian witness. How did Paul want the Colossian Christians to prepare themselves for witnessing through all the personal contacts of their lives? (Col. 4:2)

What did Paul ask the Colossian Christians to do for him to strengthen his witness through all the personal contacts of his life? (vv. 3, 4)

How are Christians to think about their contacts with other people in order to be effective witnesses for Christ? (v. 5)

WORD WEALTH

Time, *chronos* and *kairos.* There are two major Greek words translated *time* in the New Testament. *Chronos* is the simple quantitative term that indicates the progress of time as reflected by the movement of a clock. *Kairos* is the more complex qualitative term that indicates an appointed time or the prime time for an event. In Colossians 4:5 Paul called on his readers to recognize the *kairos* times for representing Jesus in word or deed to those who need to know Him.

How are Christians to manage their speech in their contacts with other people in order to be effective witnesses for Christ? (4:6)

FAITH ALIVE

What matters should you pray about in order that your witnessing by life and word would become more effective?

How can you train yourself to be more conscious of the opportunities in ordinary contacts with people around you to represent the Lord in word and deed?

What do you need to do to make your pattern of speaking more gracious and more oriented toward the Lord?

1. *Spirit-Filled Life Bible* (Nashville, TN: Thomas Nelson Publishers, 1991), 1821, "Truth-in-Action through Colossians: Key to Godly Relationships."

2. Ibid., 1910, "Word Wealth: 2:9 chosen."

3. Ibid., 1820, "Truth-in-Action through Colossians: Steps to Dynamic Devotion."

4. Ibid., 1818, "Kingdom Dynamics: Husbands and Wives Called to Operate in God's Order."

Lesson 13/Jesus: Supreme in Forgiveness
(Col. 4:7–18 and Philem.)

Seven-year-old Susie was missing, and that's all that mattered. The family vacation at a Montana campground in June 1973 turned into a vigil for the Jaegers as search parties combed the countryside and dragged the river. As the days passed, Marietta Jaeger discovered her anguish turning into rage, until she could imagine cooly killing her daughter's abductor with a smile on her face.

A man called police and demanded ransom, but he would never agree on how to make the exchange. As anxious weeks became despairing months, Marietta Jaeger recalls, "I argued and argued with God and really had a wrestling match. I gave God permission to change my heart. I began to pray for [the kidnapper] every day, which initially was the last thing I felt like doing."

A year after Susie's disappearance, a wire service ran a follow-up story on the unsolved crime. The kidnapper saw it and called the Jaegers. "It became clear he was calling to taunt me," Mrs. Jaeger said. "But in spite of the fact he was being very smug and very nasty, to my own amazement, I realized that I was feeling genuine concern and compassion for him."[1]

Police captured Susie's abductor and discovered that he had murdered her shortly after snatching her. Then he committed suicide in police custody after plea bargaining for life imprisonment.

Marietta Jaeger didn't set out to forgive this man, and she can never forget what he did to her daughter, but she had asked God to change her heart. That made all the difference between a bitter spirit of vengeance that would have poisoned her memory of Susie and a spirit of forgiveness that is free to smile through the tears.

LOVE THE FAMILY OF FAITH

An act of disloyalty and betrayal had occurred in the community of the Colossian church. Paul addressed the forgiveness of this offense in his epistle to Philemon, but you will better understand the appeal made in that letter by first examining the context of warmth and brotherliness of the church reflected in the final verses of Colossians 4.

What services would Tychicus and Onesimus perform for the Colossian church? (4:7–9)

What makes it surprising that Paul commended Onesimus so highly to the Colossians? (Col. 4:9; Philem. 10–18)

What does the presence of an enthusiastic greeting from the Christian leaders of Jewish birth with Paul in Rome imply about the congregation at Colosse? (4:10, 11; see Acts 19:29; 20:4; 2 Tim. 4:11)

What does the dedication of Epaphras to the believers of the church in the Lycus valley imply about the Christian community in Colosse? (Col. 4:12, 13; see 1:7, 8)

What does the affection shown by Gentile Christian leaders with Paul in Rome imply about the Colossian congregation? (4:14)

Keeping in mind that Colosse was a minor town and Laodicea a major city, what does the brotherly interplay between the Colossian and Laodicean churches say about the Colossian believers? (4:15–17)

 FAITH ALIVE

The Colossian congregation was known and highly regarded by prominent Christian leaders from far away and by leaders from close by. That sort of reputation is of great worth. (Compare the Laodicean reputation some thirty years later in Revelation 3:14–22).

What do you think is the connection between a concern for people and a willingness to forgive?

What do you think is the connection between a disinterest in people and an unwillingness to forgive?

LOVERS MAKE THE BEST FORGIVERS

When Paul sent Onesimus, a runaway slave, in the company of Tychicus (Col. 4:7–9) back to Philemon his master, he counted heavily on Philemon's role in creating the warm fellowship of the church. Philemon loved people; therefore, he was more likely than most to exercise Christ-like forgiveness toward the former slave who had betrayed him. The letter to Philemon is a personal note, so it is probable that the people mentioned in verses 1 and 2 are a family: husband, wife, and son (see Col. 4:17). From what is said in these verses, what kind of people were they?

What was the content of Paul's prayers for Philemon? (vv. 4–6)

In thanksgiving

In intercession

What was the great source of joy and consolation for Paul with regard to Philemon?

Which characteristics of Philemon indicate to you that he would tend to be a forgiving Christian man?

  FAITH ALIVE

Philemon and his family were pillars in the Colossian church which probably met in their house (Philem. 2). Their prominence in the church was based on loving service rather than power or control.

If an outside observer were going to describe how you treat people and influence the life and ministry of your church, what would he report?

Positively

Negatively

How do you think this imaginary observer would assess your spiritual potential as a forgiver of someone who had seriously and intentionally offended you?

AFTER ALL, HE'S FAMILY

Love is the climate that encourages forgiveness, but family relatedness is the soil in which forgiveness flourishes. When Philemon went to greet his guests who had arrived from Rome with messages from the apostle Paul and saw that one of them was his runaway slave Onesimus (Philem. 16), what emotions must he have felt? Could he ever see a brother in Christ standing there instead of seeing a treacherous thief?

On what did Paul refuse to base his plea for Onesimus? (v. 8)

On what basis instead did Paul choose to appeal to Philemon for Onesimus? (v. 9)

How would Paul's mention of his imprisonment add an emotional flavor both to his appeal and to Onesimus's status as a slave? (vv. 9, 10, 13)

 BEHIND THE SCENES

Slavery in the Greco-Roman world was an unquestioned part of the social order. Almost all labor, skilled and unskilled, was performed by slaves, and many functions we would think of as professional, such as teaching, were frequently carried out by slaves. Slaves in dangerous and strenuous settings like mining and galley rowing lived harsh and brutal existences. Field slaves experienced the rigors of agricultural life. The larger the estate, the more impersonal, demanding, and harsh conditions tended to be. Household servants in many cases experienced easier lives, and the most capable household slaves rose to positions of power as estate managers, scribes, and educators. The most prominent slaves were more literate and educated than their masters.

Legally slaves had no personal status under Roman law. They were property like animals and could be mistreated or executed on a whim. Slaves were obtained as captives in wars, were purchased from slave traders who pirated people from unprotected areas in the provinces, and were born into slavery.

Apparently Onesimus stole from Philemon (v. 18) and ran away to Rome where slaves made up an overwhelming majority of the population. Somehow Onesimus ran into Paul; perhaps he looked him up when his money ran out. Paul, who had no silver or gold, offered Onesimus eternal life in Jesus, and Onesimus discovered true freedom.

How did Paul describe his relationship with Onesimus? (vv. 10–13)

How did Paul say that Philemon would find that Onesimus had changed? (v. 11)

BEHIND THE SCENES

Slaves sometimes received names that were functional rather than personal. *Onesimus* meant "Useful" and was the equivalent of being named "Handyman." In Philemon 11 Paul made a wordplay on Onesimus's name. By stealing (v. 18) and running away, Onesimus had proved useless. Now Paul claimed that Philemon would find Onesimus to be very useful.

What had Paul wanted to do with Onesimus? (vv. 12, 13)

Why had Paul returned Onesimus to Philemon? (vv. 12–14)

What revolutionary idea did Paul present to Philemon about responding to his slave Onesimus? (vv. 15, 16)

If Philemon accepted Paul's spiritual challenge in verses 15, 16, what effect would this have on the likelihood of Philemon's forgiving Onesimus?

FAITH ALIVE

Guidelines for Growing in Godliness (Philem. 8–16). Sharing Jesus with others gives us a deeper insight into our inheritance in Christ. The godly person is immediately available for restored relationships. Practice instant forgiveness of those who have offended you. Make room for the restoration of broken relationships.[2]

FAITH ALIVE

Children can be intensely loyal to their brothers and sisters, standing up for them and taking care of them. But children can also be intensely hateful to their brothers and sisters, treating them with contempt and total disregard for their feelings. Familiarity breeds both loyalty and contempt. In the church we too often act like children toward our spiritual brothers and sisters.

What is there about spiritual brotherhood and sisterhood that should promote forgiveness among Christians?

Why do Christians sometimes treat their spiritual brothers and sisters with contempt and disregard for their feelings?

Make a list here of people (believers and nonbelievers) whom you should forbear or forgive because Christ has forgiven you (see Col . 4:13).

Those you should forbear (who have annoyed or offended you)

Those you should forgive (who have intentionally treated you badly)

Ask God for grace to obey the Lord Jesus in forbearance and forgiveness. Forgiveness is not easy. You may forgive in stages, or you may think you have forgiven an offense only to find out that you were offended more deeply than you realized and your forgiveness must reach deeper as well.

THE MANY FACES OF FORGIVENESS

In Algebra I the textbook said,

$$\text{If } A = B,$$
$$\text{and } C = B.$$
$$\text{then } A = C.$$

Spiritual calculations say,

If Paul is in Christ,
and Philemon is in Christ,
and Onesimus is in Christ,

then Paul, Philemon, and Onesimus are spiritually equal. Within the body of Christ, the many faces who need forgiveness all wear the image of Christ.

In what two ways did Paul ask Philemon to consider Onesimus and him (Paul) to be equal? (vv. 17–19)

1.

2.

BEHIND THE SCENES

"Repentance often requires restitution, which Onesimus was likely unable to make or guarantee. Paul offers to pay [Onesimus's debt and] intensifies his commitment to repay by personally writing his IOU on behalf of Onesimus. Yet, beyond this, Paul was counting on the appreciation and character of Philemon."[3]

What did Paul expect to happen if Philemon chose to forgive like Christ and chose to see Christ in Onesimus? (vv. 20, 21)

How would the presence of all the witnesses to Paul's appeal for forgiveness of Onesimus probably affect Philemon's response? (vv. 22–25)

FAITH ALIVE

If a Christian intentionally and wrongly offends you, repents, and asks your forgiveness, what should your response be?

Forgiveness is an important theme in all of the prison epistles (Eph. 4:32; Phil. 4:2, 3; Col. 3:13). What does each of the following prison epistle themes teach you about the need to forgive those who intentionally offend you?

The mystery of the gospel is that Christ has made one body out of Jews and Gentiles.

Put off the old man and put on the new.

Let your speech always edify others and never tear them down.

The power available for daily living is the power with which the Father resurrected the Son.

Let the mind of Christ teach you humility.

Follow the godly example of those who sacrificially serve others.

Christ has defeated all the powers of darkness.

Put on the whole armor of God so you can stand against the wiles of the Devil.

1. Rob Schneider, "3 Who Have Been Touched by Murder," *The Indianapolis Star,* May 30, 1993, A1.

2. *Spirit-Filled Life Bible* (Nashville, TN: Thomas Nelson Publishers, 1991), 1869, "Truth-in-Action through Philemon: Guidelines for Growing in Godliness."

3. Ibid., notes on vv. 18, 19.